THE GIFT OF MULTIPLE SCLEROSIS

Living Fully And Joyfully
Without Depression

LINDA MOKEME

Mokeme Publications

The Gift of Multiple Sclerosis

Copyright © 2017 by Linda Mokeme

All rights reserved.

ISBN-13: 978-1-7321605-0-7

Dedication

This book is dedicated to my mother, Earon Ann McGill. She is my greatest inspiration.

Her last words were:

"Watch over Linda. She is special"!

Disclaimer

This book is not intended to provide medical advice, or in any way attempt to practice medicine. It is not intended to replace personal medical care from a licensed health care practitioner. Doing anything recommended or suggested in this book must be done at your own risk. This book is the true story of the author, dates, names, locations, and actual events may have been changed.

Acknowledgements

I would like to thank Mark Hamilton the founder of the Neothink Society. My Neothink journey empowered me to share my story with fully integrated honesty. Thank you, Joel Bauer for all the value you empowered me with, regarding writing my autobiography. Thank you for helping me with my book cover. Thank you to Robert and Kim Kiyosaki for creating the board game Cashflow. Financial intelligence played a significant role regarding me completing my life story. Thank you, Kevin Trudeau, for giving me a hand up to become a member of the Global Information Network. Thank you, Kerry Asay, for bringing Tahitian Noni Juice to the marketplace. Thank you Victor Little and Bill Crane for helping me create my book cover. Thank you to my sisters Teresa Carson and Shirley McGill for always having my back. Thank you Debra O'Brien for being a very supportive friend.

Table of Contents

Prologue... ix
Chapter 1 *Name her Joy*.. 1
Chapter 2 *Mom and Dad*... 7
Chapter 3 *Mom's Breast Cancer DX*................................. 12
Chapter 4 *High School Years*... 17
Chapter 5 *College*.. 28
Chapter 6 *Back Home*... 32
Chapter 7 *Mom's Final Days*... 39
Chapter 8 *Living in Des Plaines*.. 49
Chapter 9 *Communications Technician*.......................... 58
Chapter 10 *Health & Wellness*.. 72
Chapter 11 *Attracting My Husband*................................... 75
Chapter 12 *The Natural Herb Hyssop*.............................. 81
Chapter 13 *Married in Nigeria*... 83
Chapter 14 *Relocating to Nigeria*...................................... 92
Chapter 15 *Living in Nigeria*.. 96
Chapter 16 *Living between two Continents*................... 104
Chapter 17 *Returning to Chicago*.................................... 107

Chapter 18 *Forced into Bankruptcy* 111

Chapter 19 *Betrayed* 116

Chapter 20 *Tahitian Noni Juice* 118

Chapter 21 *Marketing Wellness* 122

Chapter 22 *Noni Instructions* 126

Chapter 23 *Introduction to RichDad* 129

Chapter 24 *The Vegan Diet* 132

Chapter 25 *The Board Game Cashflow* 138

Chapter 26 *The Neothink Society* 148

Chapter 27 *Your Wish Is Your Command* 153

Chapter 28 *Confirmed MS Diagnosis* 161

Chapter 29 *Qi Gong* 173

Afterword 201

Endnotes 205

Prologue

I stood on the elevated platform on Tuesday, October 5, 1999 waiting for the Evanston Express train. Mildred, a woman I had met earlier that day in an Access Fundamental Class turned to me and said, "I see you writing". I was impressed with her insight. I had just recently been working on my book. I was curious to hear more regarding her prophecy.

She said, "You have a book in you". I shared with her that I was encouraged to write a book by a professional Bee Keeper, Mr. Sting. I met Mr. Sting while vacationing in Los Angeles in June 1995. He wanted me to write about my experience of overcoming the adverse effects of Multiple Sclerosis. He treated MS patients by stimulating them with bee stings.

Mildred said she knew other people with Multiple Sclerosis and still others who have been to Africa. She said that my book involved giving of myself along with my unique personality. She believed "The world will profit from your personality". Thank you, Mildred for sharing your integrations because when I returned to my apartment the words flowed like an endless stream.

During that same period a famous Chicago music teacher, Dr. Lena McLin was one of my Health & Wellness clients. She is an accomplished composer and music mentor who has an impressive student portfolio.

Her students include well known Rhythm & Blues music icons. When I delivered products to her house one day, she said you have a book in you.

LINDA MOKEME

She said I needed to start with my African experience. As you will see my experience with Multiple Sclerosis and with Africa is included here.

I cultivated a passion to communicate through writing early in my life. During elementary school I was a recognized author of poetry. From a very young age, I had a passion for expressing myself through writing.

Communicating through writing has always been my strongest gift. Along my journey, I got further and further away from my gift of writing. Life got in the way… love, networking, the rat race, health issues, you name it…

From the beginning of my MS journey the following biblical verses resonated in my mind:

2 Chronicles *16:*

12 And Asa in the thirty and ninth year of his reign was diseased in his feet, until his disease was exceeding great: yet in his

13 disease he sought not to the Lord, but to the physicians.

14 And Asa slept with his fathers and died in the one and fortieth year of his reign.

15 And they buried him in his own sepulchers…

After witnessing my mother's devastating experience with breast cancer, I decided to step out in faith. I chose an alternative route to Health and Wellness. What did I have to lose? I am thankful and grateful to share with you my journey.

THE GIFT OF MULTIPLE SCLEROSIS

John 10:10

The thief cometh not, but for to steal, and to kill, and to destroy: I am come that they might have life, and that they might have it more abundantly.

1

Name her "Joy"!

I was born on leap year day, 1952 in Chicago's Cook County Hospital. My proud parents were Emerson Sr. and Earon Annie McGill. A beautiful Negro female nurse encouraged Mom to name me Joy. Mom was in a state of total bliss during her entire pregnancy with me. I did not learn my middle name was Joy until I was in the first grade. My teacher, Ms. Sims asked her students to state their full names. When my turn came I said my name was Linda Ann McGill.

Mom's name was Earon Ann and my sister's name Shirley Ann therefore I thought my middle name was Ann. My teacher let me know my answer was wrong.

That evening after school I asked Mom about my middle name. She said my middle name was Joy. I was not happy! Mom's middle name was Ann. My sister Shirley's middle name was Ann. Why was my middle name different? Mom told me the story of the beautiful nurse she had when I was born. The next day my teacher made me write my full name one hundred times on my notebook paper.

LINDA MOKEME

I experienced my first birthday party on Wednesday, February 29, 1956. It was leap year day! Our apartment was colorfully decorated with balloons and crepe paper. My birthday cake had four candles. We played musical chairs, spin the bottle and pin the tail on the donkey. All the fun activities made it a memorable event.

I let Mom know I was sad because I did not get a birthday every year. She assured me the day would come when I would appreciate being born on leap year day. She said I would never get old.

We lived in an apartment in the Harrison Street projects during the first years of my life. At age five, I had a crush on a neighbor's son, Matthew. We were the same age. He was bronze complexioned and very handsome. I told Mom I had a crush on him. I was extremely shy, so Matthew never knew about my crush.

One day, I strutted proudly into our living room while Mom and dad were entertaining guests. I was boldly flaunting my body wearing only a slip. That is the moment my Dad decided I would not be allowed to date.

I was always extremely sensitive. One day during my early childhood I was traveling by railroad train to Tennessee with my mother. I cried all the way. I was missing my dad. He was not traveling to Tennessee with us.

I got lost the first time Mom allowed me to walk home from school without her supervision. I was with Helen, my classmate. I was the one who made the choice to walk in the wrong direction. We were crying hysterically when a female stranger asked us what was wrong.

Through sobbing tears, we told her we were lost. Thank goodness, Helen

THE GIFT OF MULTIPLE SCLEROSIS

knew her home phone number. The stranger called Helen's parents. Both sets of parents came to get us.

My first bestie was a white girl. Her name was Faye. We were best friends. She had wavy blond shoulder length hair. We shared everything. Every morning, I would stop at Faye's apartment building, so we could walk to school together. Some mornings I went inside. I was invited to eat breakfast with Faye and her mother.

One afternoon, Faye and I were in the girl's bathroom washing our hands when suddenly the bathroom doors swung open. Five white girls bullied their way into the bathroom. One of them was a curly red hair freckled face girl. She was our classmate, Sue. Sue and her bully friends circled around Faye and me.

Sue demanded Faye leave the bathroom with her group. She said their parents forbade them to associate with "niggers". Without hesitation Faye joined them. She followed them out the bathroom. It was my first experience with "racism".

Suddenly, I was alone in the bathroom experiencing the extreme pain of loss. It was a stab in the back. I was rejected because of the color of my skin. Time stood still as the tears poured out of my eyes and down my face. I wiped my face dry. I could not believe what just happened. I was unable to wrap my brain around it.

I slowly walked back to class. I was in a zombie state with the experience etched into my mind. At recess, I stood alone in a corner of the playground. I observed Faye playing with her new friends. We never spoke again.

LINDA MOKEME

When I was age six my parents told me, Mom was expecting a baby. It was a girl. I was happy! I was going to have a baby sister. One of my classmates a Spanish girl was named Teresa. I liked the name Teresa. I persuaded Mom to name my baby sister, Teresa.

During my youth I suffered frequently with tonsillitis. My tonsils were always swollen. I experienced many visits to the doctor's office with tonsillitis issues.

As time progressed, I became aware my parents had marital problems. One day I witnessed my dad standing at the kitchen table holding a knife. My parents had been fighting. My dad's white shirt had a blood stain on it.

I became hysterical whenever I heard my parents arguing. I would cry hysterically.

By third grade, I had acquired a passion for writing. I enjoyed writing poetry. I wrote articles for the school newspaper. I was the newspaper editor. My teacher introduced me to the famous Negro poet, Gwendolyn Brooks.

THE GIFT OF MULTIPLE SCLEROSIS

Baby Linda Joy

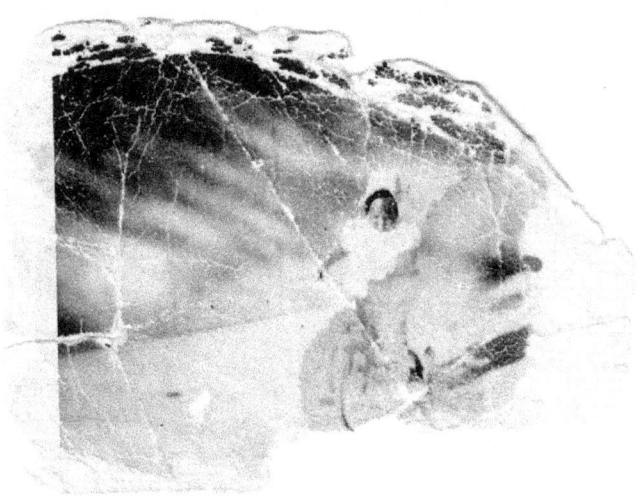

Linda with brother Emerson, Jr.

LINDA MOKEME

Mom, Dad, Emerson Jr. & Teresa

2

My dad was married three times. Mom was his second wife. He was still married to his first wife, Helen when he moved to Chicago and married Mom. My dad was forced to leave Tennessee because of his experience with whites living there.

He moved to Chicago because he had a brother Charles, who lived there.

My dad remained extremely close to his family members throughout his life. He was an excellent provider. He would proudly show off his achievements whenever he had guests in our home.

Although he had very little traditional education he was extremely talented. He was a Navy veteran. He ran his home with strict military discipline.

I do not remember ever meeting my dad's father but was told he was a carpenter. I remember only visiting his mother once. I was a young child. She was lying in bed ill. She was a beautiful Indian woman with long silky black hair. My dad's mom made her transition shortly after our visit.

I spent a lot of quality time at my Aunt Ammie and Uncle Charles' house. They lived in a middle-class neighborhood in Chicago's south side.

LINDA MOKEME

My Aunt Ammie and Uncle Charles favored me. I always enjoyed the time I spent with them.

Uncle Charles and my dad had the same father but different mothers. Uncle Charles and Aunt Ammie did not have any children. They cherished my visits with them.

My Aunt Ammie was beautiful. She was a light-complexioned amazon. Her bluish-silver gray hair glowed. I dreamed of the day my hair would be silver grey like my Aunt Ammie.

She worked as a salesperson at an upscale women's clothing store located in downtown State Street. Uncle Charles was a porter for the railroad. I learned decades later that he was in the same Masonic lodge with a very successful Negro magazine publisher.

Aunt Ammie and Uncle Charles recognized early on that I was "apt". They wanted to raise me. They wanted to help cultivate my potential. Unfortunately, my Dad was not having it. He chose to raise his own children.

Uncle Charles encouraged my passion for Art. He encouraged me to choose a mate who shared my passion for Art. My Aunt Ammie and Uncle Charles were my very first mentors.

THE GIFT OF MULTIPLE SCLEROSIS

My Aunt Ammie & Uncle Charles

LINDA MOKEME

I was a serious tomboy. I loved gym class and my gym teacher loved me. He was a Negro who favored me. He chose me to be the gym class leader. He wanted to adopt me. I was good at sports. I loved playing softball, soccer, volleyball... I enjoyed every aspect my gym classes.

One day a female classmate came to school wearing eye glasses. She looked pretty wearing glasses. I wanted to look pretty, so I asked Mom to buy me a pair of eye glasses.

Mom rejected my request. She said eye glasses were worn to correct your vision. She said I did not have vision problems. I was very upset! I screamed out, "I wish I was blind!"

That afternoon, I went to the neighborhood park to play softball. I was the catcher behind home plate. One girl slung the bat when her turn came at bat. The bat flew directly towards me and hit me in the head. I saw birds and stars.

My face was massively swollen. It was black and blue.

My left eye was swollen shut. The next day when I went to school my teacher sent me home. She said she could not stand to look at me.

Being a tomboy, I intentionally did not fight girls. I believed I would hurt them. One day I picked a fight with another tomboy. Big mistake! She gave me a beating. I never picked a fight again.

We lived in Rockwell Gardens. One day, I was in the project's playground playing "kick ball". I was wearing flip flops. I kicked hard at the ball. I missed the ball and hit the ground instead. I broke my big toe. It was dangling on my foot.

THE GIFT OF MULTIPLE SCLEROSIS

Tomboy, Linda Joy

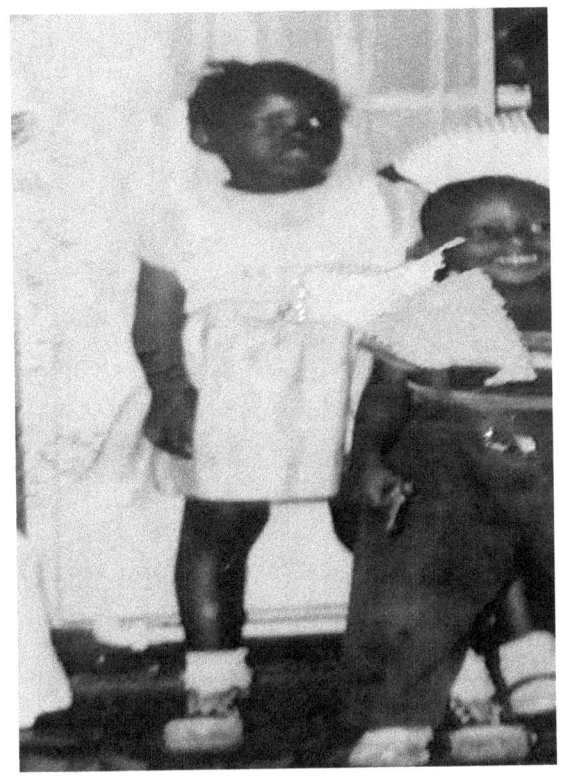

3

Mom was diagnosed with breast cancer when I was eleven years old. She had a mastectomy. She was thirty-one years young. That experience negatively affected my family life. My parent's relationship went downhill from that point on. My dad abandoned Mom emotionally throughout her remaining years.

One day, I went to a movie theatre in our neighborhood with a group of girls. I was sitting in the dark theatre when suddenly I felt a hand in between my thighs. The hand moved up my thighs until it reached my private area.

I experienced an erotic ecstasy as the hand played in my vagina. Captured by the feeling I never tried to see who my predator was. I never told anyone about the experience.

From that moment on I craved that feeling. I would stay home alone masturbating in my bedroom closet. One day I was masturbating in my bedroom closet when my dad came home.

I remained still as he walked through our apartment. When he believed he was the only one home he made a phone call. I heard him talk ro-

THE GIFT OF MULTIPLE SCLEROSIS

mantically to whoever was on the other end. Oh My God! My dad was cheating on my mother!

My dad had only three years of formal education. Yet, he was promoted through the ranks within Chicago Housing Authority (CHA). He started as a janitor. When my dad retired from Chicago Housing Authority he was an Assistant Superintendent.

Several women in our neighborhood pursued him. He was a BMW (black man working). He was a rare commodity in our community. One of the fringe benefits of his job was we lived in the housing projects rent free.

Mom was a beautiful light-skinned woman. She had an hour glass figure. I longed to look like her. Unfortunately, everyone said I looked just like my dad. I thought it meant I looked like a man.

Some of our male neighbors were attracted to Mom. It was well known that my dad was a womanizer. One neighbor, Mr. Butler was bold regarding expressing his attraction to Mom.

Mom was a housewife. Once my siblings and I were school age she began working as a maid. She worked for a maid service which was located in Chicago's Marina City Twin Towers.

Both of my parents were sharp dressers. Their first priority was their children were well-dressed. Mom dressed sharp daily to go to her maid job. She carried her maid uniform in a garment bag.

One of Mom's male clients tipped her generously. She saved the money she earned. She used her savings to put a down payment on a home for our family.

LINDA MOKEME

Mom

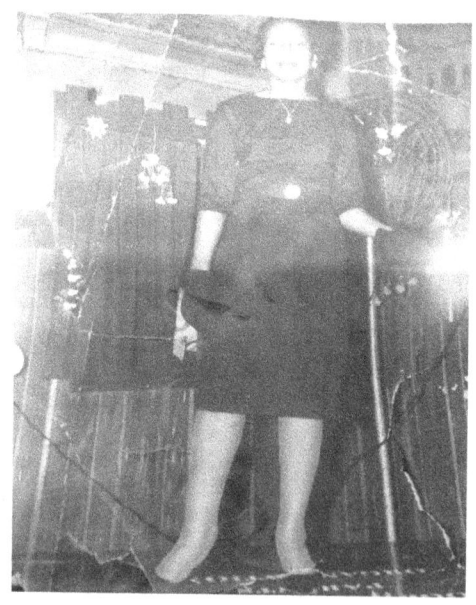

Mom

Dad

Mom & Dad socializing at home

LINDA MOKEME

I attended Crane High School on Chicago's west side. I was a member of the National Honor Society. I was in the upper top 10 of our class of 1969. There were eight hundred students in our senior class.

Starting with my freshman year my Algebra class teacher, Mr. Ornstein, had me competing against the smartest male in the class. Mr. Ornstein was Jewish. The smartest male student was Steve. I would always win the competition.

Steve was light-complexioned and handsome, yet I was not attracted to him. He had a crush on me. He consistently flew paper airplanes across the classroom towards me.

Steve was in my Geometry class. Mr. Ornstein continued to compete Steve and I against each other. One day, Mr. Ornstein contacted a major Chicago newspaper to let them know that all the books at our school were raggedy. The article was featured on the front page. After the article was published our school received brand new books!

I joined the high school chorus. I was excited about the opportunity to learn to sing. Unfortunately, my enthusiasm was short lived. The chorus teacher kicked me out of the choir. She said I was very loquacious. In my excitement I talked a lot to the students sitting near me. That was the end of my singing aspirations.

My dad was unrelenting regarding his decision to not allow me to date. Therefore, I became a bookworm. One Christmas evening, my parents were in our living room entertaining friends. My sister, Shirley and my brother Emerson Jr. were out on dates. Yet, I was in my bedroom studying my math book.

I overhead my Dad in the living room bragging to his friends about me. He told them I was extremely studious. It was Christmas Day and I was alone in my bedroom studying math. I felt like a freak! My dad assured me there would be plenty of time for dating once I achieved my scholastic goals.

A tall handsome Negro man was attracted to me. He had relatives that lived in our project building. He visited them frequently. He was 28 and I was 14. He aggressively pursued me but that was not happening.

Mr. Ornstein bragged about me to one of the high school counsellors, Mr. Johnson. Mr. Johnson was a tall slender white male. Mr. Ornstein shared with Mr. Johnson that I dreamed in color. Neither of them dreamed in color therefore they said I was special. All my dreams were in color.

My sister, Shirley was a hall guard in our high school. Her post was always surrounded by male admirers. She and her best friend Bonnie were chased home regularly from school by female bullies.

THE GIFT OF MULTIPLE SCLEROSIS

I learned from their experiences that being attractive was a liability. I intentionally dressed as a geek. I wore mixed match clothes, floral tops with plaid bottoms… I went out of my way to look like a nerd.

I met Daniel at a dance at my high school. It was a Friday evening. I had never seen him before. He did not attend our high school. He was a student at St. Mel Catholic High School. We were instantly attracted to each other.

Daniel was a fair complexioned, medium height teen. We were the same age. His handsome face was enhanced by a well-trimmed mustache. Daniel had a passion for playing basketball. He shined in the guard position. He had a large family. They had a total of eleven siblings. His family lived in a three-story brown-stone building. It was located two blocks from my high school. Daniel had a beautiful singing voice. He sang to me often. He serenaded me with the songs "My Girl"; "The Tracks of My Tears" and other Motown hits. He was extremely nurturing towards me. He placed me on a pedestal. It broke my heart when I learned he had moved in with the family of another girl. She was pregnant with his baby.

For Trigonometry class we had a different math teacher, Mr. Washington. Mr. Washington was a bronze medium build Negro man. He wore round metallic eye glasses. He had an infectious smile and his eyes twinkled.

The first day of class Mr. Washington asked a question from what we learned in Algebra. As I tried to remember the equation Steve recited it instantly. It was the correct answer.

Our entire classroom of students was in awe!

What had just happened! Steve shared that he had a photographic memory. He could remember a newspaper article he read the day before, word for word. From the moment on I never tried to compete with him.

A private school recruited Steve during our junior year. He was transferred during the middle of our junior year. I never saw him again. My classmates who lived near him told me he went to Dartmouth College. After college he was ab assistant to a high-profile politician in Washington DC. Steve was his right-hand man.

I befriended an older woman, Yvonne. She lived on the same floor of our project building. She was an attractive thick fair-skinned Negro woman. She was single, yet she had five children. Each child had a different father.

Our next door, neighbor Rita had seven children. She was on welfare. She would take her daughters to the welfare office with her. She was preparing them to be welfare mothers.

One of our teenage neighbors, Michael, shot and killed his best friend. They had argued about Michael's girlfriend. He was out of jail awaiting trial when I befriended him. He shared with me that individuals in our neighborhood would kill you over a nickel. His friend had tried to steal his girlfriend!

Mr. Ornstein took me under his wings during my entire high school experience. I was in his Calculus class during my senior year. I scored high on my ACT math test. I ranked in the top two percent in the nation.

Mr. Ornstein insisted I take typing during my last year. Typing was not a prerequisite for my college preparatory curriculum, yet he insisted I take the class.

THE GIFT OF MULTIPLE SCLEROSIS

I had already accumulated enough credits to fulfill my college prep requirements. Mr. Ornstein insisted I take typing to fill the void in my schedule. It was his solution to me not having idle time during the school day. His mission was to keep me off the streets of Chicago's west side.

Linda at a National Honor Society luncheon

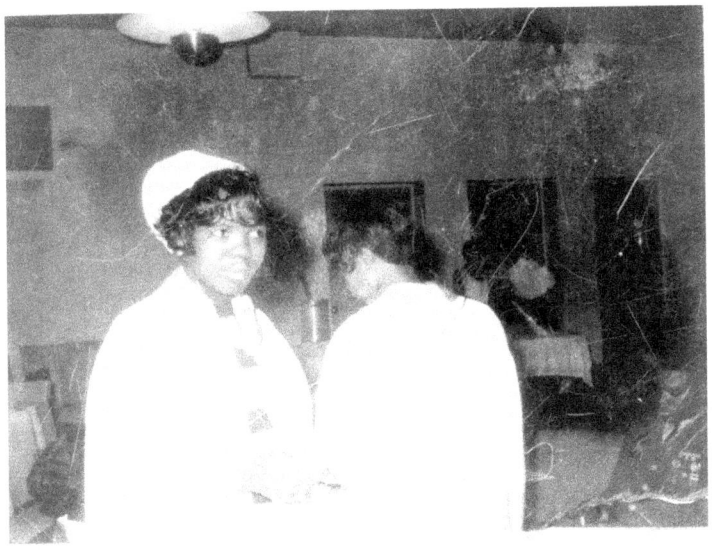

LINDA MOKEME

Mom at National Honor Society event

Receiving a National Honor Society award

THE GIFT OF MULTIPLE SCLEROSIS

I met a male named Tony at my part-time job. I worked at Allied Radio Shack during my senior year part-time after school. Tony was an attractive light–complexioned Negro male. His primarily objective was having sex with me. It never happened! As I prepared for my prom Tony volunteered to be my date.

I purchased my prom dress and all its accessories with the money I earned working at Allied Radio Shack. When prom night came I looked stunning in my peach gown with matching satin pumps. I accessorized my outfit with long white gloves, an evening purse and a tiara. My hair was combed up into a cluster of curls.

I completed the outfit with a faux stole which I borrowed from my sister Shirley. Unfortunately, Tony never showed up. He never even called. I was devastated. My dad volunteered to escort me to the prom, but I chose not to go.

One afternoon, during my senior year a male student, Allen walked me home from school. Paula a classmate who lived in my building saw him walking me home.

The next day at school she could not wait to tell Allen's girlfriend Renee he had walked me home. Renee was our high school bully.

Paula requested Renee not let me get away with it. She told Renee that my sister and I were known for stealing your boyfriend.

Paula was jealous because she had a crush on Lucas. He lived in our building. Lucas was tall and good-looking. He was my sister Shirley's boyfriend.

LINDA MOKEME

Dressed for High School Senior Prom

THE GIFT OF MULTIPLE SCLEROSIS

Renee was antagonistic towards me from that point on. She threatened to cut me with a knife. I prayed I would graduate without getting my face cut.

One day, I walked through the neighborhood surrounding my high school. I was with my best friends, Barbara and Brenda. We were cutting our afternoon classes. It was a sunny afternoon. I was wearing a new brown suede jacket, a brown knit sweater and a bright yellow wool skirt. I was strutting proudly. I purchased everything I was wearing with money I earned working at my part-time job.

As we approached a boarded up vacant building, I noticed a large group of pigeons perched at the top of the building. They were sitting on the edge of the roof. As Barbara, Brenda and I passed the vacant building suddenly there was a downpour of feces.

It felt like it was raining feces. Neither Barbara nor Brenda were affected by the falling feces only me. Barbara turned to me and said, "You are full of shit!" Completely soaked with feces, I went home and showered. I washed my hair and put on clean clothes.

Barbara, Brenda and I were inseparable. We were together at every opportunity. Barbara and I were shocked when we learned Brenda would not graduate with us. I never saw Brenda again.

LINDA MOKEME

Linda & Mom

Linda's High School senior picture

THE GIFT OF MULTIPLE SCLEROSIS

Linda's High School Graduation picture

Shortly after I graduated, we moved into a home on the south side of Chicago.

One heartbreaking memory embedded in my mind is of my fragile mom. She was standing at the back door of our home one Friday evening begging my dad to take her with him. He rejected her request and proceeded pass her out the door.

I watched him walk through our backyard to his luxury car. It was parked behind our garage. He got into the car and drove away.

5

I earned a Pullman Foundation Scholarship. It covered a portion of my college tuition. My math teacher Mr. Ornstein, had prepped me to attend an Ivy League College. I wanted to go to the all-female school – Radcliffe College. My dad rejected my college choice because it was too far away.

My dad never experienced traveling in an airplane and had no desire to. He needed for me to attend a college he could drive to. My parents decided I would attend the University of Illinois – Champaign/Urbana. They decided I would be my sister Shirley's roommate. Shirley was in her sophomore year at the University of Illinois. The campus was only a two-hour drive from Chicago.

I have sometimes wondered what my life would have been if I had attended the college of my choice. Beginning my freshman year, the University of Illinois – Champaign initiated a special program. It started a special program for black students to attend its campus.

I began school at the University of Illinois – Champaign/Urbana on August 22, 1969. From the beginning of my first semester, Lenny, a thug from East St. Louis aggressively pursued me. He asked about my sex life.

THE GIFT OF MULTIPLE SCLEROSIS

I let him know I was a virgin. He responded, "That is like having a new red sports car and not driving it".

Lenny invited me to visit him in his dorm room. During my visit to Lenny's room he raped me. I was devastated! When I returned to my dorm room, I quickly undressed to take a shower.

I wrapped a white towel around my body and hurried to the shower room. In the shower, I scrubbed my body hard. I wanted to cleanse myself of Lenny. My heart was broken. My days of proudly wearing my round virgin pin were over.

Lenny was extremely sensitive when he saw me again. He persuaded me to visit his dorm room again. I accompanied him to his room after our dorm's Sunday dinner. He forced me to have sex again.

When I returned home for Christmas break, my dad was the first to recognize I was pregnant. My parents decided I would have an abortion. They made the choice because they wanted to give me a second chance. When Christmas break ended Mom cautioned me to stay away from Lenny. She said if he talked too much he could ruin my reputation.

Lenny stalked me when I returned to campus. I was socializing with friends in the bowling alley one evening when suddenly, he appeared. I immediately left the bowling alley. I was accompanied by a male student, Jim who was gay.

Lenny followed us to Jim's car. Jim and I jumped into the car. Lenny stood in front of the car pointing a gun at us. I begged Jim to drive away. Instead he let Lenny into the car.

Jim drove me to my dormitory. During the ride to my dorm I learned that Jim and Lenny were both from East St. Louis. They knew each other. Jim was able to defuse the situation before I arrived at my dorm. I jumped out of the car and ran into my dorm.

My sister and I did not get along as roommates. I stayed out of my room as much as possible. I hung out in the dorm's lobby playing "bid whist". One of my friends from high school Dora enjoyed beating me at "bid whist". I played "bid whist" repetitively until I became a winner.

I spent very little time studying. I would wait until the last minute to study for an exam. I soon discovered college was a lot more challenging than high school. I could no longer breeze through an exam.

My best friend Barbara's fiancé, Roland attended my same college. She was a student at a different college. She would stay in my dorm room whenever she visited her fiancé Roland on our campus.

One Saturday morning, my sister and I were on our way shopping at a department store. Barbara was in town visiting her fiancé. She was in my dorm room as we prepared to go shopping. She asked me to bring her a bottle of nail polish. She did not give me any money.

I pocketed a bottle of nail polish at the department store without paying for it. A white security guard followed me out of the store and requested for me to stop which I did. He requested I empty out my pockets where I had the nail polish. My sister was not aware I had stolen the bottle of nail polish. Yet, we were both arrested.

We were finger printed and our mug shots were taken. We made the one phone call to my mother. After the phone call we were locked up in a cell.

THE GIFT OF MULTIPLE SCLEROSIS

My parents called my Aunt Lori who lived in Champaign to let her know we were in jail. My Aunt Lori came to bail us out of jail.

My dad drove to Champaign for our Monday morning court appearance. The judge let us off with a warning. That was the beginning and end to my criminal behavior.

One evening while walking through our college campus a friend and I passed by an Asian party. It was held in a facility in the middle of the campus. Through curiosity we stood by the entrance to look inside. The Asian students managing the door welcomed me to attend but rejected my black female friend. The two of us continued walking through the college campus.

I hung out regularly with my friend Dora. She was dating a soldier at the nearby Airforce base - Rantoul. One evening we hosted a party for the soldiers at Rantoul.

I cleaned and cooked twenty pounds of chitterlings. Our menu included chitterlings, spaghetti, coleslaw and hot sauce. Afterwards Dora and I hung out in her boyfriend's room.

By the end of my first year I was on probation. That was the final straw. My Dad refused to spend any more money on my college education.

When the semester ended my dad drove my sister and I home permanently. Shirley resented the fact she she was forced to drop out of college because of me.

When I returned home, I reconnected with my high school sweetheart, Daniel. Our relationship immediately escalated to the next level. Hot and bothered, we had sex at every opportunity. We were often intimate in the basement of my parent's home. I was pregnant again. This time an abortion was not an option.

During the early stages of my pregnancy, Daniel gave me a venereal disease - gonorrhea. The penicillin shots the medial doctor injected into my body caused me to miscarriage. One Friday evening I experienced extreme pains in my stomach. My mother instructed me to go to the bathroom and sit on the toilet. As soon as I sat down on the seat the embryo fell into the toilet.

My first full-time job was at Sears & Roebuck. A few months later, I switched to a government job. Working in the clerical department of a welfare office I befriended a co-worker Sharon. Sharon was a very attractive light complexioned amazon.

She was street wise and dating a successful businessman, Willie. Willie was very flamboyant. He drove an Excalibur. He also owned a Cadillac convertible. Sharon included me in her inner circle. We hung out daily at night clubs after work.

On one occasion, I was extremely depressed because my mother was scheduled for another major surgery the next morning. Sharon invited me to go to go out for the evening with her and her male cousin Billy. Billy was a professional golf caddy who was in town visiting from Florida. Sharon convinced me it would be a good diversion. Hesitantly, I agreed to go out with them.

At the nightclub, I noticed white particles in my drink when I returned to our table from the women's bathroom. I chose not to drink any more of it. I thought it was odd when Billy and his friend Jesse drove Sharon home first. The nightclub where we entertained was located on the south side. I lived on the south side. Sharon lived on the west side.

After dropping Sharon off Billy pulled his car into an alley. His friend Jesse got out of the car. At that point Billy raped me. When Billy exited the car pulling his pants up Jesse attempted to get in the car. Thinking fast, I locked the car doors. I tried to drive away. At the time, I had never driven a car.

What happened after that is buried deep in my subconscious mind. All I can remember is making out a police report and being examined at the hospital the next day.

That experience motivated me to learn how to drive every car man manufactured. I bought my first car before I learned how to drive. It was a brand-new bronze color Ford with a white vinyl top. I ran into a brick wall the first time I drove it.

Mom's tragic life initiated my Health and Wellness journey. I questioned the universe regarding why some people live long healthy lives while others suffer with health issues from a very young age.

I attended church services seven days a week. It helped me cope with the stress of my mother's terminal illness. I taught the women's Sunday school class. The minister, Pastor Blair, was teaching his Sunday school teachers one Saturday and asked if we had ever seen an angel.

He had taught us to open our mouths and let the words flow. I stood up and opened my mouth. The words "every time I look in the mirror I see an angel" came out. I was embarrassed by my response when Pastor Blair applauded stating it was the correct answer.

I was soul winning with Pastor Blair door to door in the projects when we visited a tenant who was blind. Pastor Blair described me to the blind man. I cannot remember his exact words, but he told the blind man he was missing the vision of a lifetime because I was a fine woman. His introduction caught me totally off guard. I was wearing a pale-yellow form fitting two-piece pant suit.

One Sunday, I returned home from church totally excited by Pastor Blair's sermon. Mom was inspired by my excitement. She stood up from her wheel chair and walked from the living room to the kitchen and back to sit in her wheel chair praising God. Wow! What had just happened?

I prayed to the universe constantly to please let my Mom live. My prayers were always answered. Mom lived extended years after I began to pray.

THE GIFT OF MULTIPLE SCLEROSIS

I was a Youth Motivator in the Chicago Inner City Schools. I was also an Junior Achievement Advisor. Both organizations provided a lot of networking opportunities for me.

During that same period a Negro salesman, Johnny, knocked on the front door of our home. He was selling personal care products door to door. I exclaimed "Praise the Lord!" It was an answer to my prayer. I needed a new hair product and he had one.

I struggled constantly regarding managing my hair. My dad was disappointed with the condition of my hair. He let me know I had hair like his mother. I purchased a jar of hair cream from Johnny.

Johnny also introduced me to their skin care product. It solved the problem of ashy skin. I rubbed it on my leg and my ash disappeared. It was not thick or greasy. I was sold!

Johnny invited me to attend their sales meeting. Attending their sales meetings sparked my passion for sales. I joined their organization. I marketed their products door-to-door while maintaining my full-time job.

I chose Chicago's South Shore high rise apartment buildings as my marketing territory. One of my regular clients had a hit record which was playing concurrently on the radio.

I was in awe of the business owner, Mr. Farrow. Watching him stand at the podium in the front of the salesroom and calm a crying baby in the audience was extremely impressive!

Of the Negro millionaires in the United States during that time over 90 percent of them were mentored by Mr. Farrow. He was very influential within the Negro community.

Mr. Farrow taught "Give a man a fish and he will eat for a day. Teach him how to fish and he will eat for a lifetime!" He taught that religious people were poor. I certainly did not want to be poor!

Mr. Farrow advised us to go door to door with a goal of knocking on forty doors a day. During his sales training meetings, I witnessed him critique individuals on his sales team. His criticism was usually consistently brutal. He critiqued individuals from all walks of life; doctors, lawyers and community leaders…

When the day came for him to critique me my knees were shaking together as I walked to the front of the salesroom. To my surprise he complimented me. He said that he wished he could fill his salesroom with individuals like me. My confidence went way up!

Although my essence opened doors I also experienced rejection on many levels. One of my businessman clients warned me not to be too aggressive. He told me some men would get the wrong idea.

I continued my aggressive marketing until I joined a Network Marketing organization, Cernitin America. One of the Negro sales leaders, Jeff pulled me aside and encouraged me to soft sell. "Let them come to you". From that point on I soft sold.

THE GIFT OF MULTIPLE SCLEROSIS

Linda Joy

LINDA MOKEME

Vacationing on the island of Aruba

7

By age 23, I was a totally independent thinker. I often clashed with my parents. One day, Mom was so frustrated with me she called me a "red-headed heifer". I wore my hair red at the time. My dad blamed me for their marital problems.

I chose to continue living with my parents because I wanted to be close to Mom. I gave her all my love to supplement what she no longer received from my Dad.

My dad's mistress called our home consistently during Mom's last years. She hung up whenever someone answered the phone. It caused Mom a lot of emotional pain. Out of the blue, my dad placed Mom in a nursing home.

My dad had good health insurance. The nursing home was in Chicago's Gold Coast. It was located on the corner of Oak and State Street. She was only 41 years of age. A few weeks later she was placed on an oxygen tank.

One Sunday morning, my women's class lesson was "Let go and let God". Mom made her transition two days later. I had a hard time letting go after that experience.

I rarely dated. After work hours I spent my evenings with Mom. She had survived cancer for over eleven years. Therefore, one evening after work, I chose to go out on a date. I had a date with a male nurse assistant, Allen. I met him at the nursing home. I thought it would be okay to miss one visit with Mom. I intended to visit her the next day after work.

I was wrong! She passed away the next afternoon. It was June 1975. I received the phone call while I was at work. I was working as a records clerk in the Accounting Department. I stood up at my desk a cried out in anguish.

Mom

THE GIFT OF MULTIPLE SCLEROSIS

My friend, Sandra believed Mom died of a broken heart. The day Mom passed five of her friends were in our living room competing for my dad's attention.

A happily married woman, Ms. Johnson from our old neighborhood visited Mom the evening before she passed. She was an evangelist minister. She prayed for Mom. She shared with me Mom's last request "Watch over Linda because she is special!"

I could not sleep after mom passed. One night, I watched a movie on television that ended with – Psalms 23.

"Yea though I walk through the valley of shadow of death I will fear no evil for thou art with me"

That scripture gave me peace…

I was devastated by Mom's transition. I do not know what I do not know but she came to me in a dream after she passed. She told me about a letter she wrote to me while I was in college. She never mailed the letter. I found the letter in her bedroom under her mattress one week later. It was surreal!

My dad threatened to make me do domestic chores when Mom passed. I moved out on my own a week after her funeral. I stopped going to church. The time had come for me to have my own personal relationship with the Creator.

Mom's nurse's aide, Allen moved in with me. I soon discovered he had an extremely dark side. He was a "hit man". His close friend, Rich was his "hit man" partner. Allen was physically and emotionally abusive. That nightmare lasted several months.

LINDA MOKEME

Hello Linda

How are you doing. I am still
worried about you. One loving thing
remember to take care of yourself
and remember that whatever I do
I want you to be a happy young
Lady. Linda I am so glad you
was able to go back to school. Tracie
was her last night asking for you
[illegible] I [illegible]
had went back to school. also
[illegible] people had asked me about you all
and said Daynia if you wouldn't
mean funny you'd be real in
an mean. you [illegible] them alots
for your age [illegible] but don't you
to look ahead and just look
and remember you are still a
young girl [illegible]

THE GIFT OF MULTIPLE SCLEROSIS

LINDA MOKEME

Hello Linda,

How are you doing? I am still worried about you over doing things. Remember to take care of yourself and remember that Mother loves you. I want you to be happy. You are a young lady!

Linda, I am so glad you were able to go back to school. Terry was here last night asking for you. Daddy said he looked surprised you had returned to school.

Also, a lot of people has asked me about you and Shirley. They seem surprised if you know what I mean. Linda your life was really in a mess. You have been through a lot for your age. But we are going to look ahead and not backwards.

Remember you are still a young girl in so many ways. You have got to live your life as any young girl has a right to. Always remember there are nice boys in this world. One day will meet a nice one but take it slow. Stay as far from Lenny as you can because he can hurt you now if he talks too much.

I want you to study hard and get good grades. We miss you but for once in my life I am glad you are at school. Oh, how I know how hard it could have been when you go through life like that. I am not saying we were right, but love is blind when it comes to seeing your kids hurt.

We want you to be happy. So now you have a second chance. Make the best of it. Remember Mom and Dad love you. Be sure to take care of yourself. You and Shirley please get along like sisters.

Love, Mother

THE GIFT OF MULTIPLE SCLEROSIS

Sharon hosted a bridal shower for my marriage to Allen. I learned after the shower he was already married.

It lasted long enough to put fear in my heart regarding living with someone else. After several months of the nightmare with Allen, a black male at my job Greg, helped me get out of the relationship. Greg had tried aggressively to date me for months. He jumped at the opportunity to help me get out of my toxic relationship. He was a trained martial artist.

Months after we started dating I learned Greg was also dating one of his female peers, Annette. They were both communications technicians. I learned about Greg's relationship with Annette when he showed up for our date one day at his home in Gary, Indiana. He was driving Annette's Toyota car. He had spent the night at her north side apartment. The next morning his black Camaro sports car was missing.

LINDA MOKEME

I asked my friend Sharon for advice regarding Greg's cheating on me. She advised me to break out his car windows. His car had been stolen. He was driving Annette's car. Following Sharon's advice, I broke out the back window of the car Greg was driving. He was driving Annette's car.

Greg believed I was insane. He ended our relationship. Greg persuaded Annette not to press charges. Not having a car to get to work in Chicago from Gary he moved in with Annette. Shortly afterwards they were engaged. They had a church wedding six months later.

Within a short time after his wedding Greg was aggressively pursuing me again. I rejected him, but I eventually gave in. I still loved him. On top of that the sex was good! Our relationship lasted for ten years. He drove from Gary, Indiana to Des Plaines, Illinois three times each week to be with me.

THE GIFT OF MULTIPLE SCLEROSIS

Greg had a passion for traveling. We traveled often. Freeport, Bahamas, Atlanta, Georgia, Omaha, Nebraska, Toronto, Canada...

He always had a reefer joint ready when he came to visit me. I had sexual inhibitions, smoking weed was the perfect aphrodisiac. It relaxed me!

The rapes I experienced caused me to be frigid. I met other men, but Greg always chased them away. One Thanksgiving evening, I was socializing at a nightclub in Chicago's Gold Coast. I was feeling good! I was wearing my hair in an extension braid style with gold ornaments mingled through the braids. I was attractively thin. I felt like Cleopatra.

One of the bouncers at the nightclub was a famous black celebrity. He observed me on the dance floor. When the dance was over he walked to my table and handed me a red rose.

When I shared my Thanksgiving Day experience with my friend, Sharon she told me the bouncer was a member of the Mafia. Greg pleaded with me not to date the celebrity. He did not want to have to have to fight him off.

Simultaneously, I continued to grieve the loss of Mom. I grieved for seventeen years. I experienced insomnia. Greg was unsympathetic. He recommended I read a book on transcendental meditation.

In 1977, when I returned home to my north side apartment two men I had dated were standing outside my apartment building. They were waiting for me. It was the sign I needed to move. I needed to live in a neighborhood that was not easily accessible.

A female real estate owner introduced me to the Rosicrucian Order – AMORC. I joined the Rosicrucian Order specifically because it was not a religious organization.

I shared with a different real estate owner, Mr. Mendel that I was a member of AMORC. He was impressed! His response was that I was a believer. He handed me the lease to his one-bedroom condominium in Des Plaines.

I chose Des Plaines because it was an affluent part of the Chicago area. I remember reading an analogy describing the city as a watermelon. The red part with the black seeds depicted the violent part of the inner city where the blacks lived. The white part with white seeds depicted the surrounding area where the whites lived. The green part was where the wealthy lived.

LINDA MOKEME

Mr. Mendel was Jewish. He was an attorney. He immediately assumed the role of my protector. His law office was in a commercial building in downtown Des Plaines.

I never had to worry about paying my rent. I paid my rent whenever I felt like it. Attorney Mendel was always there for me.

I worked in Rolling Meadows in AT&T's accounting department. I experienced racism on a whole new level. I found out whites lived outside the city because they did not want to live near blacks.

The few that I worked with were openly racists. They played favoritism to further exhibit their racism. They favored the black employees who they could control. I have always had my own mind which presented a problem. They labeled me as a "troublemaker".

Most of the neighbors in my condominium community treated me like I was invisible. Once during a snow storm someone slashed my car tires.

One of my co-workers poisoned a plant I had on my desk. When I went to water my plant soap suds appeared. Through it all I focused on remaining solvent. I was suspended for one week because I made a long-distance phone call to Gary, Indiana from a company telephone. It was a less than five-minute call.

THE GIFT OF MULTIPLE SCLEROSIS

Dancing with my father

After continuous problems with my Ford, I traded it in for a brand-new Volkswagen Jetta. It was a stick shift. I had never driven a stick shift before. I was involved in a car accident within a few weeks after I purchased it. I was stopped at a light and shifting gears on Golf Road in Skokie, Illinois when a car rear ended me.

I passed the Communication Technician examination test with flying colors. My managers gave me a song and a dance! They blocked me from getting a promotion by giving me a low appraisal rating. They wanted me to take an additional test. When I shared the information with my tax accountant he told me not to take another test. He said they were playing games. I chose to follow my tax accountant's advice.

Eventually I was promoted to a Service Representative. My new job was in Schaumburg, Illinois. I was a student at Oakton Community College. As I continued my education my managers gave me more and more challenging job responsibilities.

In 1981, AT&T sold an Electronic Tandem Network (ETN) system to Moore Business Forms. The order requested eight hundred tandem circuits to be ready for service on the same due date. AT&T managers believed I could do anything. Therefore, in March 1982, I was "chosen" to be the dedicated Service Representative for the ETN project.

It was the largest Electronic Tandem Network in telecommunications history. I attended Local Exchange Company (LEC), meetings and participated in unlimited conference calls as the sales team aggressively coordinated the project.

THE GIFT OF MULTIPLE SCLEROSIS

Linda on a "road trip" to Atlanta

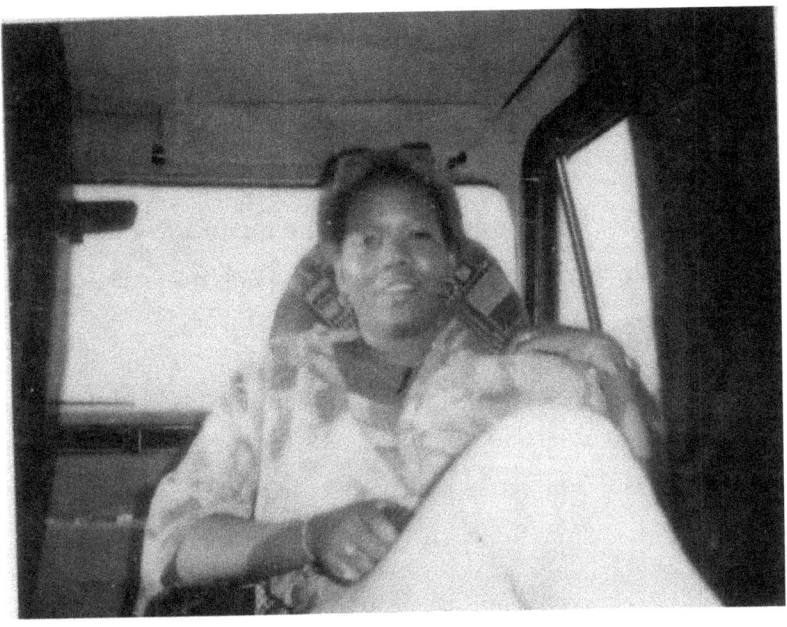

LINDA MOKEME

I turned up the eight hundred ETN circuits to the client on the due date -Complete as Ordered. Several years later an AT&T Salesman confided in me that servicing the Moore Business Forms Electronic Tandem Network was a hardship. He said he would rather have AIDS.

Unfortunately, the stress of the massive ETN project expedited the growth of a fibroid tumor in my body. The tumor grew exponentially. It weighted over twenty pounds and was choking my uterus. It caused excessive bleeding and blood clots.

When I consulted a medical doctor, he recommended immediate surgery. I chose to get a second opinion. I received a letter in the mail from the first physician. The letter had blood on it. A friend from Farrow Products introduced me to her natural physician, Dr. Finley.

I went on a supervised twenty-day fast to reduce the tumor. I lost a lot of weight but not the tumor. I was extremely thin, yet my stomach looked like I was five months pregnant.

After I consulted with five physicians Dr. Finley recommended her medical doctor, Dr. Townsend. I immediately felt secure with, Dr. Townsend. He was also a minister. His clinic was in the Cabrini Green projects neighborhood. During my first visit he quoted a bible verse. Proverbs 3:6 *"In all thy ways acknowledge him and he shall direct your path"*. It gave me peace.

Dr. Townsend was medium height brown-skinned charismatic man. His proud stance made him appear much taller than his actual height. His medical peers described him as a genius. I chose to let him perform exploratory surgery. He prayed and held my hand as I was rolled into the surgery room.

THE GIFT OF MULTIPLE SCLEROSIS

The first question I asked Dr. Townsend when I regained consciousness was how soon I could have sex again. He backed away from me saying he not want to get struck by lightning. He was aware of my relationship with a married man.

The exploratory surgery ended up being a partial hysterectomy. My ability to carry a child was ended. That reality spiraled me into a deep depression. Thoughts of how I had been in a relationship with a married man for a decade daunted me. My dream of having a daughter was destroyed.

Dr. Townsend approved additional time off from work, so I could heal psychologically. They started a rumor at my job. They said I was having an affair with my doctor because he approved the extended medical leave.

My already delicate body was further damaged when I was in an automobile accident in 1983. I was the passenger as Greg drove from my condominium in Des Plaines, Illinois to the Baha'i Temple in Wilmette, Illinois. Driving east on Golf Road just as we entered Evanston, Illinois the car behind us slammed into Greg's car and knocked us into the car in front of us. We were not wearing seat belts.

Attorney Mendel introduced me to Attorney Mair. He trusted him to represent my personal injury case. Attorney Mendel was getting older and did not have the stamina to do the leg work required for my lawsuit. Attorney Mair was a younger Italian man.

THE GIFT OF MULTIPLE SCLEROSIS

9

I was working in downtown Chicago on a temporary assignment when I was finally promoted to Communications Technician. The managers of the engineering department at my temporary assignment were extremely pleased with my work. They decided to keep me in their department indefinitely.

My Schaumburg managers authorized my promotion to Communications Technician when they realized I was not returning to their office. The Communications Workers of America (CWA) our employee union attempted to block my promotion. They wanted to use me a pawn to negotiate promotions for other employees they represented.

I had requested the CWA's help in the past regarding my promotion issues with no success. I was not receptive to working with them regarding my pending promotion.

Working in the communications technician capacity, my white female supervisor, Patty was jealous of the attention I received from my male peers. She consistently micro-managed me. She gave me a workload eight times the size of my male peers.

She forced me to work a lot of overtime hours running jumpers on the main frame at the telephone company's central office. As I stood on a

THE GIFT OF MULTIPLE SCLEROSIS

ladder soldering circuits on the main frame, one of my white male peers continuously shocked me with an electric rod. He would catch me off guard and shock me with the electrical tool.

One evening, after working long overtime hours I drove a coworker home. As I arrived at her house I could not feel my left foot when I stepped on the brake pedal. I thought it was a sign I was extremely tired. I was working a lot of overtime hours, yet I drove my coworker home. We lived in opposite directions of the city.

One freezing cold morning, I was running cables on the main frame when I answered a phone call. When I put the telephone to my ear I could not feel my face. I thought it was frostbite. I called my boyfriend, Greg and told him what I was experiencing. He insisted I call my Doctor. When I called Dr. Townsend he scheduled an appointment to see me in his office immediately.

The next morning, the entire left side of my body was paralyzed. It was the day before Thanksgiving. I woke up on Thanksgiving Day 1984 in St. Joseph Hospital paralyzed on the entire left side of my body. I instantly became angry with the world. All the adversities I had experienced finally got the best of me.

I experienced an infinite number of tests, electric shocks to my wrists, spinal taps, an CRT, an MRI… After two weeks of extensive testing I was transferred into a room with an individual who had lupus. She was diagnosed as having Lupus several years before we met. She shared her experience with Lupus to prepare me for my new health status.

She shared her experience with depression which included being on her pity pod. She encouraged me to keep up my physical appearance emphasizing looking good makes you feel good.

After two weeks, I became discouraged because I was not getting any answers. I signed myself out of the hospital. I was not happy! I decided I needed to be at home. When I returned home I discovered someone had broken into my car. I still owned a Volkswagen Jetta. They stole my Panasonic FM/AM cassette player.

Having a mathematical mind, I believed there was a solution to every problem. I did not get any results at the hospital. When I returned home my neighbor reminded me I had always been extremely positive. He encouraged me that the same attitude would help me regarding my paralyzed situation.

Dr. Townsend, my supervising physician called me at home to check on me. My family questioned my sanity. Thank goodness, I have always been a self-leader, so I continued my journey uncontrolled.

After a few visits to my neurologist's office I was uncomfortable moving forward in that direction. I perceived his objective was not to help his patients get well. He offered his diabetic patients candy bars. One of his patients at his clinic was wearing a colostomy bag. Yet the doctor encouraged him as he ate a bologna sandwich. This contradicted with my beliefs regarding wellness.

I chose to take an alternative medical route to wellness. I left traditional western medicine and chose holistic medicine.

Mom had a tragic health life. She had rheumatic fever when she was a child. She was diagnosed with breast cancer when she was 31 years young. I witnessed her deterioration from being beautiful and voluptuous to a frail woman who was incapacitated. I decided I had nothing to lose by choosing an alternative route. My Health and Wellness journey began with me visualizing myself traveling and living my life full out. Watching Tina Turner perform on television inspired me.

Reading Tony Robbins "Unlimited Power" motivated me.

Sitting in my condominium apartment, I stared at the oil paintings on my walls. I focused specifically on my oil painting of an ocean scene. It gave me peace!

Reviewing my MRI pictures Dr. Townsend was impressed with the size of my brain. He showed me the MRI. He said it gave him confidence in my ability to think. I told him I had decided to pursue alternative medicine.

He supported my decision and recommended his chiropractor Dr. Doran. I made an appointment with Dr. Doran whose clinic was in Lisle, Illinois. Dr. Doran x-rayed me in February 1985. He told me to get off the prescription drug Prednisone immediately. He told me its side effects were worst, then an actual disease. He adjusted me three times a week. With the help of his treatments and electronic therapy I was walking again.

When my employer learned that I was no longer under the care of a medical physician they scheduled an appointment for me to see their corporate medical physician. Their physician scheduled me to return to work.

He documented me as "Fit for work - Light duty". My supervisor put me on a light duty desk job. He demanded I schedule an appointment with my original physician to get an official medical release.

In my Des Plaines condo-apartment shortly after I was paralyzed.

THE GIFT OF MULTIPLE SCLEROSIS

My neurologist was impressed with my progress. He told me my test results were positive for

Multiple Sclerosis. I was devastated by the diagnosis. I had never heard of Multiple Sclerosis. I would have been more comfortable with a cancer diagnosis. At least I was familiar with cancer.

I called my close friend Sharon. She was the first person I told about my MS diagnosis. I was hysterical. She encouraged me to think positively.

Sharon was very supportive. She drove me to networking events whenever I wanted to attend them. Some events were three hours away. Sharon helped me get to the next level. I was feeling good!

When I shared the diagnosis with my Chiropractor, Dr. Doran. He assured me that I did not have MS. He said that I was a mess, but I did not have MS. He discouraged me from doing any research on Multiple Sclerosis. He said that I had subluxation degeneration. He continued to adjust me three times a week.

When I shared the MS diagnosis with my employer, they worked aggressively to get me off their payroll. A friend, Sherri who was an Human Resources executive at another telephone company told me the story about an employee who was fired because she had MS.

Multiple Sclerosis caused her to take an excessive amount of days off work. Being self-sufficient I was petrified! How would I survive? I needed a way to earn income from home. I was single, disabled and fighting to remain solvent. In March 1985, I went to see Dr. Finley. She recommended natural herbs to help me get better. They tasted terrible and were extremely bitter.

LINDA MOKEME

Linda at Disney World – 1985

THE GIFT OF MULTIPLE SCLEROSIS

I did not have a choice, I had Multiple Sclerosis. That began my journey with nutraceuticals (natural medicine). Along the way, I learned that the body has an innate ability to heal itself given the right food.

On my way to my Chiropractor's clinic in Lombard, I visited an attorney friend who lived near the clinic. She and her husband were successful investors. They sponsored me into their Network Marketing organization.

I listened to her because she was my high school classmate. She and her husband were successful. It was the answer to my prayer. I needed a home-based business. I promised the creator if he would let me walk again I would use my sales essence to help others with their health issues.

Network Marketing was the solution to my problem. All the information I needed to rebuild my health came through networking. It was fun. I met a lot of interesting people. They shared their wealth of knowledge.

My Christian chiropractor encouraged me to change my lifestyle. Before my paralysis I hung out with friends smoking reefer. I tried snorting cocaine shortly before I woke up paralyzed. My boyfriend was a user.

Dr. Doran prayed for me and read bible verses as he adjusted my body. He insisted I forget about positive thinking and focus on the word of God.

Looking on the bright side, Multiple Sclerosis slowed me down. Attorney Mendel told me even with MS condition I had more energy than the average person. I had a reputation of being fast. Simultaneously the AIDS epidemic had just begun. I went to work and returned home. Reading and working on my home-based business became my only focus.

LINDA MOKEME

Linda at Networking Marketing event.

THE GIFT OF MULTIPLE SCLEROSIS

In 1986, I changed to a vegetarian diet. I was a Communications Technician working at a desk job. A white male peer, Larry who was 23 years old started taking a lot of time off work due to the stress of his job responsibilities. He was going bald. My white female supervisor, Donna took Larry's job responsibilities from him and gave them to me. All my hair fell out.

I was attacked on the job in an elevator by two Illinois Bell male employees. They were black. One was married yet he wanted to have sex with me. I was fighting off the two men when the elevator opened, and a white male employee got on. I exited the elevator on the very next floor.

During that extremely sensitive situation, I was psychologically abused by a white female AT&T counsellor. She said that she was an attractive woman yet that had never happened to her. She told me I brought it upon myself. I experienced racism, sexism and jealousy in the workplace.

When Attorney Mendel retired he invited me to come to Greece with him. He was a short older man and he was not attractive. I visualized what people would think when they saw us together. I felt they would believe I was a gold digger. I chose not to accept his opportunity.

LINDA MOKEME

Linda when all her hair fell out.

My friend, Sandra thought I was insane not to take advantage of Attorney Mendel's opportunity. She wished she had the same opportunity. Her sister Pamela who lived in California was well provided for by wealthy individuals. Pamela was a Piscean like myself.

I thought the world of Attorney Mendel yet my gut told me not to accept his offer. He sold his real estate properties and relocated to Greece. He instructed the new owner of my condominium to provide the same care I was accustomed to.

A few years later Sandra was diagnosed with breast cancer. She had a mastectomy. She became extremely bitter. She was jealous of me because

THE GIFT OF MULTIPLE SCLEROSIS

I did not have a visible illness. Her doctors gave her five years to live. I loaned her $150.00 to buy a special bra. Although, I was not concerned about the money she stopped speaking to me because she did not repay the debt.

By that time, Sandra had two young daughters. She was overwhelmed. She was diagnosed with cervical cancer a year later. By 2000 she was diagnosed with rectal cancer. She made her transition shortly afterwards.

I met a female podiatrist, Dr. Jordan while attending church in the Gold Coast. She was African American. She had a head full of long, thick and beautiful hair. She shared with me her secret regarding having healthy hair.

LINDA MOKEME

Captured in 1985 - I was managing two Models. We were in the middle of a photo shoot.

THE GIFT OF MULTIPLE SCLEROSIS

I wore a wig for several years due to baldness. When my hair started growing back I was ready for a change. My job was killing me. I spent my evenings crawling on my living room floor in crippling pain.

It was during that time in my life that I discovered the powerful effect music had on me. An attorney friend, Laura, had invited me to a social event which was on after my work day on a Friday. I was exhausted from a demanding week at work. I was sitting in a corner dozing off when a charismatic figure entered the room. It was Stevie Wonder! Suddenly I was alert and full of energy.

10

During the summer of 1986, I met a new associate, George. We attended an event at the AMORC lodge in Chicago. He was a sharply dressed Nigerian. He was an Information Technologies (IT) specialist. He was a vegetarian.

He exposed me to my first Health & Wellness convention. The event was in Rosemont, Illinois. George took me to the next level of my Health and Wellness journey.

I was exposed to a lot of alternative health products and resources. After the experience, I attended Health & Wellness events within the Chicago area repetitively. I chose alternative over traditional medicine.

Through networking at the Natural Health events, I learned "You are what you put in your body." I purchased and read the books "You Don't Have to Be Sick" and "Health to the Millions". They promoted Natural Hygiene. I learned the value of eating a natural diet with salad as the main entrée. I discovered that the body is addicted to foods as well as drugs and alcohol.

The body needs the proper amount of rest and fresh air. Proper ventilation is important to good health. Wearing natural fabrics, cotton, silk, wool, leather anything natural allows the skin to breathe. Synthetic clothes are not healthy for you.

Linda in Manhattan, New York at an AMORC event

LINDA MOKEME

I learned it is important to keep air circulating in your homes throughout the year. Always have a window slightly opened in your residence.

I attended a seminar where the speaker informed us that the AIDS virus was created in a laboratory in the United States…

.

11

I was 40 years old and single. I was successful, yet I was lonely. I lived alone in Des Plaines for seventeen years. I was the only African American in the condominium complex almost the entire time. After years of being isolated in an all-white environment I had the desire to be married.

Throughout life we are brainwashed with illusions regarding love, Cinderella, Rapunzel, Sleeping Beauty… Inspired by childhood romance stories I was excited because I believed I had met my "Prince Charming". He was a Christian. He attended church services regularly. I believed he was a Saint.

I remember the first time I saw him. I was attending an AMORC event during the summer of 1988. He was sitting on the other side of the room. He was charismatic and debonair. I thought to myself "There he is! That is my husband"! After the speaker's presentation, I watched him standing in the hall outside the seminar room. He was surrounded by a group of white women.

I decided to focus on my itinerary for the day. Preparing for the dinner dance that evening, I dressed in my finest attire. I applied information I learned from reading the book "How to Dress to Attract a Husband".

Dressing for the dinner dance I chose my purple knit designer top and a brown leather midi skirt. I cinched my waist with a wide brown leather belt. My leather pencil skirt was form fitting! I accessorized my outfit with brown leather pumps and layers of silver jewelry.

When I returned to the five-star hotel I saw him again. He was standing in the lobby. He had just returned from a tour of Chicago. This time he went out of his way to meet me. Ironically, a gentleman I had dated in the past George introduced us. George is the Nigerian that I had met at the AMORC lodge a decade before.

His name was Emanuel. He lived in another state. He had just returned from a tour of Chicago which included visiting the Hard Rock Cafe. After our introduction he excused himself to go to his room and get dressed for the evening gala event.

I sat at a table with a group of my African friends. Emanuel entered the banquet room looking like royalty. He wore a white tuxedo jacket and black tuxedo pants. He walked directly to our table and asked permission to sit in the chair next to me.

From that moment on we were inseparable! He was Nigerian and an internationally celebrated poet. He lived in Minneapolis, Minnesota. He was employed in the medical industry. He was a vegetarian. I enjoyed talking with him.

After dinner the DJ played Marvin Gaye's "Let's

Get It On". Emanuel invited me to the dance floor. He held me close. I was in my sweet spot! An African American woman who was born on the west side of Chicago had finally met her "Prince".

THE GIFT OF MULTIPLE SCLEROSIS

He invited me to his hotel room where he told me about his business background. He showed me his elegant clothes in the hotel closet. One of his white male roommates returned to their hotel room. Emanuel impressed both of us with stories about his business experiences.

Emanuel and I walked through the hotel gardens as I left to drive home for the evening. I returned to the convention early the next morning. It was Sunday and the last day of the event. Emanuel invited me to lunch. I drove to my favorite Pizza restaurant in Evanston. On the way to Evanston I stopped at my condominium.

He was impressed. I drove a Cadillac. I lived in a condominium in the suburbs. The condominium had a sliding window which led to a balcony. I had two of everything, two color televisions, two VCR's, several oil paintings, a barbeque grill on the patio… I was the epitome of a material girl.

At lunch Emanuel massaged my arm. I felt his energy flowing through me. When we returned to the Marriott his roommates were already in the parking lot. Four white men were busy positioning their suitcases into the trunk of the car.

I received a greeting card in the mail two days later. It was from Emanuel. He called me daily. I was thankful his visit to the Chicago was short lived because I knew it could have escalated to an intimate experience quickly. Over the phone we had the opportunity to become plutonic friends. The man I was dating at the time was legally blind. He sensed there was someone else. I denied it. Emanuel and I were just plutonic friends. Emanuel invited me to Minneapolis to visit him a month after we met. He promised it would be a strictly plutonic.

LINDA MOKEME

Linda on airplane flight to Minneapolis.

THE GIFT OF MULTIPLE SCLEROSIS

We were unsuccessful regarding connecting at the Minneapolis airport. I took a cab to his address. When he finally returned home, we were not in his apartment ten minutes before our relationship escalated to an intimate level. We were standing against the wall and heavy into the act when his doorbell rang. One of his friends had accompanied him to the airport. He was following up regarding their search for me.

Emanuel catered to me all weekend as I visited him in his self-contained studio apartment. He cooked breakfast. We went window shopping in an upscale neighborhood. We ate lunch at a Chinese restaurant. He took me dancing at a popular Minneapolis night club. Afterwards we socialized with an intimate group of his friends.

6 weeks later my relationship with my other man terminated due to my "missing in action" weekend. Simultaneously, I was being pursued by a younger man, Willie who worked in my department at work. Willie was bow-legged and extremely good-looking. He was ten years younger than me. By now Emanuel was insanely jealous in Minneapolis. I was in heat and sexually on fire. I begged Emanuel to come to Chicago to visit me.

The weekend Emanuel was scheduled to come to Chicago he broke his leg. I was hot and bothered when Willie called on Friday evening. He invited himself over. I warned him it at his own risk stating he might get laid.

It was already late that night and Willie lived over an hour away in a far south suburb. Therefore, he made plans to visit me the next day. He arrived early Saturday evening. Teddy Pendergrass was playing on the radio when I seduced him in a dance.

The next thing I knew we were driving to the big chain grocery store located two blocks from my apartment to buy condoms. That was an experience to remember! We had sex for eight hours straight. We continued our sexual marathon the next day.

Thank goodness that Monday was a scheduled day off because I could barely walk. Willie returned a few days later for an encore. We had sex frequently, Willie was a serious freak! Simultaneously, I exposed Emanuel to the speaker Tony Robbins book "Unlimited Power". Emanuel attended a Tony Robbins event in Minneapolis. Applying what he learned from Tony Robbins, Emanuel was "winning"!

Emanuel's life improved for the better which caused jealousy on the part of his immigration investigators. They went out of their way to have him deported. He was arrogant and proud. He boasted of his elite lifestyle in Nigeria. He was not intimidated by their threats.

Emanuel was forced to leave America when the woman he married withdrew her immigration papers. He never lived with her. He invited me to come to Nigeria with him, but I was shocked to learn he was married.

When he left the country, I was still dating Willie. I was whipped! ! I was an official member of the "cougar" club and loving it! Willie consistently took our sexual experiences to the next level.

The turning point came when he wanted me to participate in a "ménage à trois". Two different women called begging me to participate in a threesome with him. That was the sign I needed to change. I began reading the bible from the beginning to the end. I became celibate, yet I continued to masturbate.

12

It was a Sunday afternoon during the summer 1990 and I desperately desired to be at home. My white female business partner, Lola persuaded me to attend a networking event with her. I was in crippling pain. I wanted to rest before the next day which was Monday, a work day.

We were at a Health & Wellness event when an African American man, Mr. Sawyer introduced himself to me. He was an entrepreneur who manufactured the Holistic Herb, "Hyssop". He said it had miraculous healing powers.

Mr. Sawyer lived in Hollywood, California. He was very generous. He paid for a group of seven to have dinner. I purchased his products solely to support an African American entrepreneur. I had no expectations! I started using the products immediately. I was surprised when I experienced instant results.

Up to that point, I had a limited lifestyle due to acute back pain. Stress, prolonged activity, typing, standing, everything caused me intense pain. I had very low energy. "Hyssop" changed all of that "Hyssop" changed all that. Suddenly I was working overtime and partying with my friends after working hours.

I was responsible for ten times the workload of my white male peers. My performance was at ninety-seven percent. Yet, I was rated less than satisfactory due to one incident with a white female client.

It was approximately the same time that Spike Lee's movie Malcolm X was playing in the theatres. I seriously considered changing my last name to X. I had experienced decades of racism. I wanted out. I was tired!

AT&T was experiencing a major downsizing. I was extremely overworked. I returned to my Des Plaines condominium in crippling pain on a regular basis. I was not living. I earned a good income. I was on call 24 hours a day including weekends. I rarely took a day off.

One evening on my way home after work I crossed paths with my first love, Daniel. He was excited to see me. He told me about a private conversation he had with Mom. She had asked him not to have sex with me.

He let me know he had been successful in the drug business. He had leveraged his money into real estate. He was moving to Miami, Florida. He asked me to come with him. By that time the thrill was gone, therefore I turned down his offer.

13

In January 1993 I received a letter postmarked Nigeria. It was from Emanuel. By that time, I was aggressively asking the universe for a husband. . I loved the Lord, but I desired a physical companion (I was the minister on top of a roof and a flood was coming!)

The letter from Emanuel was the answer to my prayer. He invited me to come to Nigeria to marry him. I literally was prepared to swim to Nigeria. I traveled to Nigeria in May 1993.

My Jewish landlord Attorney Mendel had prepared me for my Nigerian opportunity. He mentored me regarding my life choices. He advised me not to travel to poor countries.

Although I had not heard from Attorney Mendel since he retired and moved to Greece his advice still resonated with me.

As a result, I was very selective about where I traveled. I did my due diligence and learned Nigeria was the richest country in Africa. I had always wanted to experience Africa for a minimum of six months. Therefore, I accepted Emanuel's marriage proposal. I also preferred to visit places where I knew someone. The invitation to come Nigeria to marry Emanuel worked for me. The time had come!

A model friend of mine Mary, and my Jewish business attorney friend, Mr. Pacini offered their advice. They advised me not to go unless he paid for it. I ignored their advice.

I agreed to marry Emanuel because I was 40 years young and I had never been married. White female peers at work encouraged me to follow my heart to Nigeria. They thought foreign accents were sexy.

One of them took me under her wings to prepare me for the immigration process. Unfortunately, nothing can prepare you for an experience with immigration.

My supervisor, a white male, tried to discourage me from going to Africa. He disliked the idea of Africans having access to technology.

I had just completed reading the Bible from Genesis thru Revelations. I asked the creator for a husband. Except for masturbating, I was celibate.

I believed "God" had sanctioned my marriage to Emanuel. I remained focused regarding my commitment to keep my mind on the Lord. I wanted to be involved in the international marketplace which was also a deciding factor.

Preparing for my trip, I went to the library to research Nigeria. What I read terrified me! During my airplane flight to Nigeria in May 1993, I befriended a female who was sitting next to me. She was Nigerian. After transferring to a connecting flight in the Heathrow Airport, London we arrived in Lagos twenty-six hours later. It was night and extremely dark outside. My female Nigerian friend stayed by my side as I looked for Emanuel.

THE GIFT OF MULTIPLE SCLEROSIS

Paralyzed with fear I could not recognize Emanuel in the massive crowd in the airport. It was filled with an enormous amount of black people. Experiencing an airport filled with black people was difficult to mentally process.

My Nigerian travel companion invited me to come home with her and her relatives. I rode in the car with one of her brothers. He explained that looking for Emanuel's address at night would be difficult and dangerous. He explained it was wiser to look for the address during daylight hours.

He travelled to America frequently. His home had the ambiance of an American lifestyle. He was a gracious host. The next morning his housekeeper cooked breakfast for us pounded jam, plantain, fish...

My hosts persuaded me to give them a chance to make sure the coast was clear at Emanuel's place. They warned me he could have another wife. My hosts were Muslims. The thought of Emanuel having another wife made me livid. How could he invite me to Nigeria knowing he had a wife?

When my cab arrived at Emanuel's address his friends recognized me immediately. He had just walked to the main street looking for me. When Emanuel returned he was beaming from ear to ear when he saw me. He carried my luggage as he escorted me to his apartment.

Looking around his studio apartment, I observed a mattress on the floor. There were boxes in the corner which contained his belongings. Several books were lined along the wall. What had I gotten myself into?

Emanuel held on to me tightly. He was aware I was celibate. Shortly after I arrived we went to visit his sister, Eunice. Eunice, her husband and children lived in a gated facility. They had guards at their front gate. She owned a Mercedes Benz car, a Mercedes station wagon, a Jeep Blazer, a Jaguar, and a Rolls Royce… Their opulent home was in an affluent community. She had domestic help and a chauffeur. She was a successful businesswoman. She had modeled internationally.

I met Emanuel's circle of friends. They too were very successful. My Nigerian experience was straight out the lifestyles of the rich and famous. At the same time, I was confused because it was not the Africa I had expected to experience. Where were Tarzan and Jane?

Emanuel told me he had been extremely ill the year before I came to Nigeria. He told me he had died and came back to life. I took it as the sign I should marry him. We were given a second chance.

I was impressed by the lifestyle Emanuel exposed me to. It was the rich lifestyle I dreamed of. Emanuel and I were just starting out. He assured me we would get there.

We went to the "black market" to exchange money – U.S. dollars to Nigerian Naira. I was overwhelmed by the abundance of Naira that the Hausa Muslim men controlled. One of Emanuel's female relatives dated a man who owned a car dealership. He lived in a luxurious mansion. We lived in a neighborhood near Allen Street. Allen Street is their elite shopping district.

I arrived in Nigeria during a Muslim Holiday. A favorite expression of the Nigerian females was "dash me". Dash me means give me something. They also referred to you as "Auntie". The Nigerian women worshipped their men. I met only a few who shared the western mindset regarding female equality.

THE GIFT OF MULTIPLE SCLEROSIS

When the Muslim Holiday ended Emanuel and I traveled to Enugu where his father was hospitalized. His father was in a coma. He had been in a coma since March. Simultaneously, the doctors at the Enugu hospital were on strike.

We traveled to Enugu by bus. The bus was the size of a mini-van. It was an experience – straight out of the movies. I felt like I was in the movie, Indiana Jones. We used the bathroom outdoors. I witnessed a female shoot her urine a distance just like a man. It had an arch. At least I thought she was a woman. She looked like a female.

We stopped to visit one of Emanuel's sisters who lived in Onitsha. She was a teacher and her husband an entrepreneur. He distributed electronic products on an international level. We stayed overnight in their apartment. She had three bedrooms and a maid. We continued our journey to Enugu the next day.

In Enugu, we stayed in the apartment of Emanuel's close friend. His friend was living in America. We stayed with his friend's wife and daughter. The husband, David, was a medical doctor in Nigeria. The wife, Kim, was a teacher. The mother-in-law was also a professional. Before she retired she taught math in England.

Emanuel introduced me to an artist in Enugu who painted beautiful oil paintings. The talented artist described one of his spiritual artworks by telling me a story about Jesus after the crucifixion.

I was bored staying in the apartment all day when Emanuel visited his dad at the hospital. I decided to accompany him. After years of hospital visits during Mom's illness I developed an aversion to hospitals.

I visited Emanuel's father in the hospital for one week. On Sunday, I prayed for God's will regarding his dad. He father passed away the next day. We were at his bedside. Emanuel was devastated.

Now he prepared for our trip to Oba which is the village where Emanuel grew up. No one could tell Emanuel's mom that her husband was dead. It would be four weeks before his funeral services were held. They put his body on ice. They needed to prepare for the funeral and get the word out. Individuals needed to travel to Nigeria from around the world to attend the services. His father was a powerful man!

I had traveled to Nigeria seeking happiness. Yet, I was in the middle of a family's painful loss. His father's passing caused widespread grieving. Emanuel's sister Eunice exemplified her father's power.

She was wealthy and lived an influential lifestyle. She was powerful! She warned me not to marry her brother if I did not plan to have children. She let me know it was their tradition to procreate.

I had made up in my mind to marry Emanuel. I had passed up the opportunity before because I knew I could not have kids. This time I was selfish! I wanted to marry him.

I would have followed him almost anywhere. I discovered the international man I had followed to Nigeria was a strict African male. Our marriage was extremely challenging for me.

I met Emanuel's other family members, his older brother was a Medical Doctor who lived in Benin

City. He was the head of the World Health Organization (WHO) in Benin. His sister, Lady

THE GIFT OF MULTIPLE SCLEROSIS

Diana looked a lot like me. Lady Diana's husband was knighted by Queen Elizabeth. He was a banker.

Emanuel was away from home during the day preparing for his father's funeral. I was alone with his mom and housekeeper at their estate. Neither one of them spoke English.

The village of Oba was remote from transportation. My one month Leave of Absence was coming to an end. I was stressed out because I did not have access to communications.

Emanuel experienced malaria. He was angry because he felt I was insensitive. One day he angrily threw a newspaper at me. His mom gestured that he had his dad's temper. Unfortunately, it was a sign of things to come. Emanuel's Mom insisted he marry me. She was impressed I had traveled to Nigeria to be with him.

In the village of Oba, Emanuel introduced me to another talented artist with art on the level of the ones you see in museums. The artist owned an eagle and a baby crocodile.

When we returned to Ikeja, Emanuel was determined to marry me before I returned to America. Being sensitive I could not break his heart. He was in mourning!

Emanuel and I argued the morning we were married. It was not a romantic experience. Yet, Emanuel continued to get dressed to marry me. I understood the emotional pain of grieving and believed in having someone be there for you.

We were married at the courthouse in Victoria Island on June 17, 1993. He promised me a formal wedding later.

LINDA MOKEME

Two days after we were married I was on a return flight to the United States. Simultaneously, Emanuel returned to Oba to finish planning his father's funeral.

THE GIFT OF MULTIPLE SCLEROSIS

June 17, 1993 –

The day I married Emanuel

14

I returned to Chicago just in time to attend my niece, Lavisa's wedding. Her wedding day was Saturday, June 21. The wedding and reception were at my sister Teresa's home, in the backyard. Teresa lived with her husband and son in a 4-bedroom home in Aurora, Illinois. It was a happy experience for my family.

What had I done? I looked around my condominium apartment. I did not know what I was going to do. I scanned newspaper ads searching for an answer. I joined a yoga class.

I was paralyzed by fear. I would have to move to Nigeria to live with Emanuel. I prayed for an answer. I received my answer in September 1993 when AT&T's Focus magazine published a carton article which featured caricatures of people throughout the globe.

It depicted individuals dressed in their native attire. To represent Africa the article displayed a gorilla sitting under a telephone poll eating a banana. Ironically, I never received a copy of that issue.

Blacks at AT&T and throughout the United States were outraged! AT&T fired the artist and discontinued the publication of the magazine.

THE GIFT OF MULTIPLE SCLEROSIS

Simultaneously, one day at work I witnessed three white females skipping through the hall singing, "Shake hands with the monkeys!" Blacks at AT&T went out of their way to bring the article to my attention. I experienced a deep pain! I was married to an African. I was a member of an African family in addition to being, a Black American.

I knew on a profound level "Why the Caged Bird Sings!" On my spiritual journey, I had learned that prosperity means never doing anything you do not want to do for money. Therefore, I had my answer.

I submitted a one-year Leave of Absence request to my supervisor the following Monday. I signed the contract with the knowledge that I was not guaranteed employment at the end of my Leave of Absence. It was approved!

I placed newspaper ads to sell my possessions. I sold and gave away material things which I treasured. I put my remaining possessions in storage. I took the things I treasured with me to Nigeria. It was an overwhelming experience.

Ironically, November 1993 was my twentieth-year anniversary working at AT&T. An African American male peer who was also a network marketer advised me to work 20 years to become fully vested before I left the company. For several years, I chanted twenty and out over and over.

When I traveled to Nigeria to marry Emanuel he showed me his immigration documents. Immigration approved his immediate return to the United States to marry a white woman. When he married me, immigration blocked his visa with my every attempt.

LINDA MOKEME

December 23, 1993 was my last day on the job. I had manifested my dream. I worked for AT&T exactly twenty years. The time had arrived to begin my next chapter.

Sitting in the living room of my Des Plaines condominium

THE GIFT OF MULTIPLE SCLEROSIS

My going away party December 1993 – moving to Nigeria.

15

On January 9, 1994, I received a call from my attorney. He told me fraud was documented on Emanuel's immigration records. He requested an additional attorney fee of $1200.00. The payment was due before I traveled to Nigeria.

Three days before my departure I had not received my airplane tickets. I had paid for them two months ahead of time. I called my attorney regarding the airplane tickets. I had three days remaining to vacate my condominium.

It was three weeks since my last day at work. My year Leave of Absence would begin in three weeks. I was experiencing a nightmare! I was forced to sell my Cadillac Cimarron.

On Sunday, January 16, 1994 it was 50 below zero and snowing when I boarded the international flight. The day had arrived! I was relocating to Africa. I arrived in Lagos, Nigeria the next day Monday, January 17. It was Martin Luther King Jr. Day in the United States.

I took an elegant designer wedding dress to Nigeria. I purchased it and all the accessories I needed to get married. I was ready for our formal

THE GIFT OF MULTIPLE SCLEROSIS

wedding. It never happened! I never saw my dress again!

I took my treasured art sculpture – Sheba to Nigeria. It was valued at $5000. Emanuel was physically abusive. He was jealous of my love for Sheba. He made me leave Sheba in Nigeria. A very successful African American music mogul is one of the few individuals that owned the same sculpture.

Nigeria is a beautiful country, yet it was consumed by corruption. I witnessed financial corruption first hand. Individuals committing fraud (411).

The men and women in Nigeria were entrepreneurs. They traveled globally for business. This was the opposite of my American experience. I favored the Nigerian business mindset.

Emanuel's friends and family were doctors, engineers, architects, air traffic controllers, entrepreneurs, lawyers, bankers… One woman had taught math in Europe. She had several degrees in science. I was extremely impressed!

Emanuel was a celebrated poet who had exceptional skills in communications. He was well groomed and polished. He was meticulous about his appearance. His influence had a direct effect on the woman I am today.

Emanuel association was high class! Our challenge was our cultural differences. I did not spend enough time with him before we were married to get to know him. I had no regrets because our union took me to the next level.

Emanuel became bitter because I was unsuccessful obtaining a visa for him. He believed I did not want him to come to America. He was not able to obtain an American visa and the economy in Nigeria was plummeting.

His friends volunteered to help me with domestic chores. Yet, Emanuel insisted I do them myself. He wanted me to learn the nitty gritty details, so I could supervise domestic helpers work more effectively. I cooked dinner by candle light. We had a gas generator because we did not have a stove oven.

I fetched water every morning using soda bottles and a bucket. I went to the marketplace three times a week to purchase food. I got down on my knees and brushed our carpeting with a hand-held broom. I cooked breakfast, lunch and dinner. I scrubbed our dirty clothes by hand. I walked or rode the bus to the marketplace. Some of Emanuel neighbors questioned if I was really an American when they witnessed me fetching water.

Being shy I have always been more comfortable expressing myself through writing. Emanuel's communication skills were a significant factor regarding my choosing him as my marriage partner. I believed we would collaborate as a team. It never happened!

I learned Nigerians were fearless. I witnessed individuals being happy with very little material possessions. The majority had no electricity nor running water.

One of us needed to travel to America to raise capital. Therefore, I had to commute between the continents to sell merchandise. I commuted between the continents every three months.

THE GIFT OF MULTIPLE SCLEROSIS

During one of my commutes I met a highly respected Natural Physician – Dr. Elizabeth Kenya. When she learned about my testimony she requested to meet me in person. Emanuel took me to her clinic. During our brief encounter she brought immense value to my journey.

She gave me an autographed copy of her Natural Healing book. Emanuel approached her regarding becoming a distributor of Hyssop in Nigeria.

After she listened to my testimony she told me I was now prepared for the "inner secrets". Dr. Kenya introduced me to a book titled "The Holy Grail"! (In the beginning was the word)!

She wanted my help to participate in the Health & Wellness Conventions in America. She needed to market her workbook. By this time my relationship with Emanuel was strained. He was antagonistic because of his immigration issues. I never saw Dr. Kenya again.

"You always maintain long distance relationships" one of my friends observed. The reality was, I was my best lover. I masturbated at every opportunity. I masturbated while reading my weekly AMORC lessons. I masturbated while reading the Bible from the beginning to end. I masturbated early in the morning and late at night. I was addicted!!!

When I commuted to America I masturbated while visualizing Emanuel having sex with another woman.

In August 1994, my third trip to Nigeria I had a surprise for Emanuel. I brought to Nigeria $11,000.00 in product inventory and $5000.00 in cash. Emanuel had bragged about what he could do with $5000.00. As soon as I gave him the money his attitude changed.

He left me stranded on the road with his friend Nick. Emanuel told me he did not want me. He took off his wedding band and threw it down the road. Nick said I should beg Emanuel. I let Nick know I had given Emanuel $5,000.00 before he turned against me.

Nick accompanied me back to my apartment. The next morning Emanuel said he had given me a "China bowl" and I had destroyed it. He said he wanted me to come close to him. He said if I came close to him no one could ever come between us. I did not understand. I was with him in Nigeria. I was giving all I had. After decades of enduring racism, I was aloof by nature.

He immediately started spending the $5000.00. He had customized furniture built for our studio. I had expected him to invest the money in business endeavors. To his credit, he designed a couch for me to sleep on. Sleeping on the couch was comforting for my back.

I am grateful I took advantage of the opportunity because I have no regrets. Living in Nigeria gave me exposure to an elite class.

Emanuel's young friend, Nancy was elegant. She had a rich boyfriend. She wore attractive form fitting clothes. She wore classy pumps.

Her dresses were below the knee. She was attractively thin and very aware of her sensuality. In contrast, I wore all black and a lot of red.

THE GIFT OF MULTIPLE SCLEROSIS

Emanuel told me he did not like the way I dressed.

Linda in her apartment in Nigeria.

My exposure to fashion in the United States was limited to the earth tones i.e. taupe, grey, navy. Nigerians wore colorful clothing made of elegant fabrics.

When I went to Nigeria I owned a wardrobe of spandex dresses. We were on our way to dinner on Valentine's Day 1994 when I was booed by a group of youths. On another occasion, I was waiting for the bus after a hair appointment when a stranger insisted I get in his car. He drove me home and warned me to dress appropriately for Nigerian streets.

Nigerian media constantly discouraged its listeners against dressing like the western culture. Nigerian women dressed refined. They wore clothes that were attractive yet with decorum.

Those are the Gifts that I am grateful for. Growing up on the west side of Chicago limited my exposure to refined dressing. Malcolm X's autobiography stressed, "You can tell the character of a country by the way the women are dressed!"

We had challenges in our sex life. I masturbated every time I was alone. One night, Emanuel retired for bed when I went to the kitchen to get a candle. Suddenly, he sent me on an errand next door.

When I returned to our apartment he was holding my candle. He was aware he could not satisfy me. That was the moment he discovered I was addicted to masturbating. He told me, I was sick! He insisted I return to America and get "delivered". I cried whenever I left Nigeria. My masturbation addiction made me very insecure.

THE GIFT OF MULTIPLE SCLEROSIS

Linda horseback riding on an Nigerian beach.

16

On my first wedding anniversary June 17, 1994, I was in Chicago. It was the day they tracked down O. J. Simpson on the expressway for murdering his wife. I watched it live on television. Was it a sign of things to come in my life?

I tried to return to my job in November 1994. It was three months before my Leave of Absence expired. Simultaneously, my managers placed a job freeze in my department. The freeze blocked me from returning to work.

In January 1995, the African American female who was the director of my department made the decision to terminate my employment. My Leave of Absence expired on February 14, 1995.

My white male supervisor was shocked. He needed me to return to work. I was an asset to his team.

I returned to Nigeria in February 1995. I no longer masturbated. By that time Emanuel's "sister" was pregnant. He was insensitive and abusive towards me. Nancy was seven months pregnant. Emanuel moved her into our new apartment.

THE GIFT OF MULTIPLE SCLEROSIS

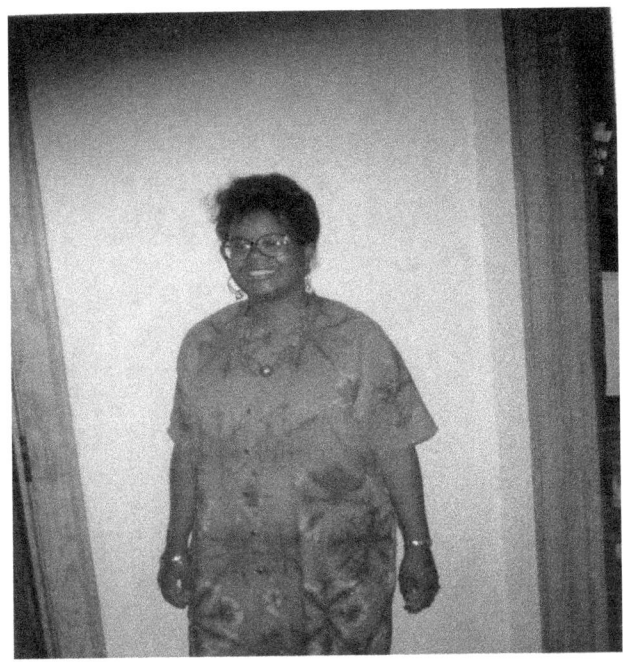

Emanuel and Nancy slept in the bedroom. She wore sexy lingerie. I was forced to sleep on the couch in the living room. It was karma for my dating a married man for ten years.

Emanuel begged me to give him a chance to return to me the right way. He put me on an airplane to the United States on June 17, 1995. It was our second-year wedding anniversary.

Emanuel talked me into sending him my last $2000.00. He said he would use it to sneak into America. The U. S. Postal Service intercepted the package and returned it to me. On essence, I began selling the herbal product Hyssop and African products in the marketplace.

LINDA MOKEME

17

In July 1995, I moved into a studio apartment on Howard Street and Sheridan Road on the north side of Chicago. The rent was $300 per month. I was unemployed. I remained solvent selling products in the marketplace.

Shortly after I moved in I discovered the apartment was infested with roaches. It did not have heat in the winter. It was the best I could do. I chose to live alone. I no longer trusted anyone.

The information in Dr. Kenya's workbook brought immense value to my Health & Wellness journey. Little did I know how our brief encounter would positively affect my life. I shared the information I learned from her workbook as I sold health products in the marketplace.

Reading Dr. Kenya's work-book I learned how harmful and unnatural masturbating is. I was faced with the fully integrated honesty of how masturbating physically and psychologically throws an individual out of balance. I learned prolonged masturbation damages the nervous system. Multiple Sclerosis is a disease of the central nervous system.

What Is Multiple Sclerosis (MS)?

Multiple sclerosis (MS) is an unpredictable, often disabling disease of the central nervous system that disrupts the flow of information within the brain, and between the brain and body.

Multiple sclerosis (MS) involves an immune mediated process in which an abnormal response of the body's immune system is directed against the central nervous system (CNS), which is made up of the brain, spinal cord and optic nerves. The exact antigen — or target that the immune cells are sensitized to attack — remains unknown, which is why MS is considered by many experts to be "immune-mediated" rather than "autoimmune." Within the CNS, the immune system attacks myelin — the fatty substance that surrounds and insulates the nerve fibers — as well as the nerve fibers themselves.

The damaged myelin forms scar tissue (sclerosis), which gives the disease its name.

When any part of the myelin sheath or nerve fiber is damaged or destroyed, nerve impulses traveling to and from the brain and spinal cord are distorted or interrupted, producing a wide variety of symptoms.

The disease is thought to be triggered in a genetically susceptible individual by a combination of one or more environmental factors.

People with MS typically experience one of four disease courses, which can be mild, moderate or severe.

THE GIFT OF MULTIPLE SCLEROSIS

Masturbating robs the natural flow of the universe. A woman needs her man's energy field and vice versa. A woman is designed to be a receiver and a man is designed to be a giver – socket and plug analogy. The plug needs a socket to connect to the energy.

I stopped masturbating in December 1994. I finally overcame my addiction. By that time, masturbating had destroyed my life. All my decisions were integrated with my addiction to masturbating. Masturbating was a form of safe sex. Yea right! It bounded me to the dark side.

By winter 1995, I worked as a fundraiser at the Art Institute of Chicago. It was a relief from my freezing apartment. We were paid on commissions only. Our job was to persuade donors to increase their financial contributions.

Abstinence from masturbating helped me achieve more as an entrepreneur. Through networking, I met Daniel Oba who was a Nigerian businessman. He was a co-founder of the African Chamber of Commerce in Chicago. He took me under his wings. He was impressed when he learned I had lived in Nigeria. He adopted me as part of his family. Nigerians referred to me as "my wife"!

I was treated special! Working in the marketplace with my Nigerian friends, I earned income to pay my bills. I was extremely thankful. My Nigerian network empowered me to keep a roof over my head.

There were times I was extremely destitute, yet I never regretted my decision. I was defrauded by Emanuel, his brother and an African American associate, Mary. They stole my money, my wedding dress, my clothes, jewelry, books, domestic products, my sculpture Sheba… They stole my dream!

Dr. Kenya's workbook was extremely valuable. It prepared me for the miracle of Tahitian Noni Juice. It helped me understand why my body was out of balance. I have long since overcome my addiction to masturbating.

Masturbating inhibited me. I was shy and withdrawn. I could not reach my potential because my private time was spent masturbating. I did not have the ability to love. I could have sex but not love.

I was thankful for my African experience, but my life was difficult. I had experienced betrayal in my marriage. I struggled to support myself. I sold wellness products in the marketplace. I relied on Dr. Kenya's workbook because all my other Health and Wellness reference books were in Nigeria.

My clients were highly educated therefore I needed effective information. When I learned the information regarding masturbating being harmful, I realized I was totally out of harmony with nature. I certainly had issues with my nervous system.

18

By July 1, 1996, Emanuel's brother and my African American associate Mary forced me into bankruptcy. Emanuel's brother charged $36,000 on my American Express Corporate Card. He sent me a fraudulent check as partial payment. Mary borrowed $2000 from me and refused to pay it back.

She filed bankruptcy and listed me as one of her creditors. My creditors pursued me aggressively. They contacted my neighbors and my dad who lived in Michigan. The debt collectors called me daily. My phone rang from 8 in the morning to 9 at night.

My business mentor, Michele referred me to an attorney. My Dad and my sister Teresa voluntarily gave me money to pay my bankruptcy lawyer. My bankruptcy was approved in November,1996. Looking out the window of my attorney's office I saw two golden angels. They were sculptures on top of the building directly across the street. I felt the presence of "Grace". I broke down in tears.

LINDA MOKEME

Linda a few days before the African Festival of the Arts 1995

THE GIFT OF MULTIPLE SCLEROSIS

I met my friend Michele through Phillip. I met Phillip shortly after I returned to Chicago from Nigeria. He was an attorney. Phillip attended an event where I was a vendor. I was with Wellness entrepreneur Mr. Sawyer. Phillip requested his Hyssop products be delivered to Michele's business. She owned a printing business. It was conveniently located. It was located on Michigan Avenue just north of Madison Street. Michele took me under her wings and invited me to many influential networking events. Our birthdays were one day apart. She was born on February 28. She had three grown children. Her only daughter was an actress. Her daughter lived in Beverly Hills, California. Simultaneously as I worked my wellness business, I also worked temporary assignments through an employment agency.

One of my many assignments was at the Salvation Army. I worked directly with the branch Director on a high priority data entry project. He needed my data entry skills to help him identify criminal activity within their organization. They were experiencing an internal theft. Working on the assignment I felt the presence of pure evil.

I quickly learned that corruption was not limited to Nigerians. We identified the criminal as the manager who I directly reported to. She did everything within her power to sabotage my success on that assignment. She stole my personal belongings. She as well as other employees which included a police officer had stolen a million dollars from the facility. She quit her job before I completed the assignment.

I had a desire to attend church but the church I was a member of was located on the far south side. Riding on the red line train from 7500 North to 9500 South I was robbed. A black male who was wearing a black hoodie snatched my gold necklaces. He caught me off guard. I was dozing off. I never rode the red line to church again.

One day while I was marketing as a vendor at Navy Pier, I met a black couple who lived in my neighborhood. They invited me to attend their church. It was located a half a block from my apartment. Before I met my neighbors, I would pass the church and ignore the urge to go in. I observed white people inside.

They were jumping up and down. At the time, I had an aversion to white people. The racism I had experienced in the past was still embedded in my mind. I discovered that greed and demons do not have a color. I attended the church every Friday evening.

The wife went back to the world three weeks after inviting me to attend their church. The couple got divorced. The husband remarried and moved out of the country. He told me he did not believe in the "Bible".

I continued to attend Natural Health & Wellness events. I met the event producer. He invited me to a private meeting. The speaker told us the dollar was going to be devalued. He said the sign of the dollar's devaluation would be the change of the face of the dollar. He encouraged us to invest in gold. At the time gold was $300 an ounce.

I shared the information with my family and close friends. Unfortunately, they did not listen to me.

THE GIFT OF MULTIPLE SCLEROSIS

Linda marketing at Today's Black Woman – 1996

19

Emanuel reached out to me in August 1996. By this time his friend Nick was living in America. Nick let me know Emanuel married his "sister" Nancy shortly after I returned to America. Luckily, I was dating a younger man, Phil from Ghana. It was the cushion I needed as I experienced my major heart break.

When I returned permanently to Chicago from Africa, I no longer had income from a job. One day in 1997 I answered a job ad on Craigslist. When I applied in person, I arrived at a high rise residential building in Chicago's Gold Coast. The white male in the apartment requested to take a picture of me naked. Wow! One of the lowest points of my life. I never told anyone. I was desperate. I needed money, so I let him take the picture. He gave me $50 in cash.

In February 1997. I learned Phil was cheating on me with a woman I introduced him to. I met her at an African Chamber of Commerce event. When I asked for her help tweaking Phil's resume she requested to meet him.

From the first encounter she brazenly went all out to impress him. She had a master's degree from Stanford. She was single. She lived in Evanston and was on staff at Northwestern University.

THE GIFT OF MULTIPLE SCLEROSIS

He had a journalism degree in Ghana. He was working on his American portfolio and he needed a green card. They betrayal me. When I called her the Sunday before Valentine's Day 1997 I heard a baby crying in the background. Phil was the father.

I called her to share my joy. I was in love with Phil. ."Silly, wasn't I?" I l found out he also had another African American woman. She was the mother of his twins. One of the twins had a heart disease. I was heartbroken and defrauded. I had recently loaned him $400. He said he needed it to obtain his visa.

Pamela volunteered to repay the $400. She wrote me a check. I went to her bank the next morning. Her checking account had insufficient funds.

That was a painful Valentine's experience for me. Thank goodness, I kept myself groomed. I went to Hyde Park for my hair appointment that week on Thursday afternoon. I learned my client Diana's sister had just passed away. She had cancer. Diana's sister was 35 years young. Life had its way of helping me keep things in perspective.

20

During the summer of 1996 I had the exhilarating experience of seeing Princess Diana. She was visiting Chicago for three days. I was returning home from the Small Business Administration center. I was on a Chicago Transit Authority bus.

We were stopped at a traffic light when the Rolls Royce that Princess Diana was riding in pulled up beside us. She was charismatic and benevolent as she smiled and waved at us. She was wearing a burgundy suit and hat.

It was the same time Prince Charles had publicly announced he never loved her. We shared a common denominator both of our husbands rejected us.

What an enchanting summer! In July 1996 Tahitian Noni Juice was introduced to the marketplace. By November 1996 a friend, Joan who worked with me at AT&T called to tell me about Tahitian Noni Juice. By the end of December another friend a chiropractor, Dr. Harper, was calling me about Tahitian Noni Juice.

I read the information about Tahitian Noni Juice and perceived it had similar properties to Hyssop which I was already marketing. I did not choose to confuse my clients. Therefore, I was not interested.

THE GIFT OF MULTIPLE SCLEROSIS

By 1997, I was struggling with chronic fatigue. Every day by 2 PM I was extremely fatigued. I was forty-two. I thought it was a sign of old age.

In February 1997, my sister Teresa had a cancer scare. I learned about her health issues three days after my client's sister passed from cancer. I reviewed Dr. Kenya's workbook. It confirmed that fruits and vegetables have medicinal properties.

"No matter the kind of disorder, the herbs to heal such is always provided by nature. …against every illness there is an herb that grows."

"Most herbs have distinct tastes and aroma. The very bitter ones are the most potent and they are known to have the ability to bring harmony between the body and the soul. Their curative properties are many and very effective." (Immense Help from Nature's Workshop – page 9.)

Trusting the information, I read in Dr. Kenya's workbook I encouraged Teresa to try natural medicine. She was open! She had a massive growth on her thyroid. Her medical doctor was recommending surgery.

On my birthday March 1, 1997, Teresa treated me to lunch at Houston's restaurant in Chicago's Gold Coast. During lunch I persuaded her to call and make an appointment with my chiropractor, Dr. Harper. He scheduled an appointment to see her the same day. We went to his clinic directly after lunch.

Using medical terminology, he explained the benefits of the nutraceutical product, Tahitian Noni Juice. Teresa invested in a case. She signed up on Case Auto-ship.

I purchased one bottle to support her decision. I am extremely frugal, therefore I had to justify the cost. It was my birthday. I applied the reasoning women pamper themselves for their birthdays. I immediately began drinking it. Suddenly, I was like an ever-ready battery.

After spending time with my sister, I went shopping with a friend, Jackie. After shopping, Jackie and I went to a restaurant for dinner. That evening I hung out with a nurse friend, Alicia. Alicia had African male friends who were visiting from Europe.

We socialized at a Caribbean nightclub and went to an African party. We partied all night until the next morning. Alicia and I accompanied her friends to O'Hare airport when they left to return to England the next morning. It was my first 24-hour experience.

I was a believer. I immediately signed up as an Independent Product Consultant (IPC) on Case Auto-ship. I was struggling to pay my bills. I did not know how I would afford my additional monthly commitment.

Two friends immediately volunteered to be my regular customers. That was three bottles a month out of a case of four. I was confident I could sell the forth bottle. Magically, individuals began joining my distributor team. I had clients for Tahitian Noni Juice all over the city.

Drinking Tahitian Noni Juice daily, I experienced a cleansing. I had acute pains in my stomach in the morning. It felt like I was in labor. Thank goodness, I was at home and near a toilet because I had to defecate. I was instantly cured of constipation. I passed gas uncontrollably. It was embarrassing!

THE GIFT OF MULTIPLE SCLEROSIS

I was healed from chronic fatigue. I overcame a decade long experience with insomnia. For the first time in decades I was sleeping like a baby. I experienced emotional well-being. My heart has

just been broken by my Ghanaian lover. That type of heart break normally caused me to fall into severe depression. This time I was feeling good! As my sister, Teresa and I compared notes over the phone the massive growth on her thyroid disappeared.

We are spiritual beings having a human experience. Therefore, it is important that we seek our true selves. Through my love for Jesus Christ and the Word of God I was elevated to a place of bliss. My faith in alternative medicine attracted Tahitian Noni Juice.

Before Tahitian Noni Juice I envied my MS clients, who were extremely disabled. They had visible signs of their illness. Although one of my clients was totally incapacitated her devoted husband who took great care of her. I regretted my life choices because no one was there to help me.

I was chronically fatigued. I could go to the marketplace to sell my products, but I did not have energy to do domestic chores. When I was first diagnosed I had a good job and could afford maid services. Now my finances were extremely limited.

21

After only a month, Tahitian Noni International sent me a check for ninety-dollars. Suddenly, I was earning retail profits and receiving commissions checks. I acquired a desire to learn how to keep this income flowing.

I learned Noni (Morinda Citrifolia) feeds the pineal gland. The pineal gland is situated in the middle of the human brain and is the major site of the body's melatonin production. I learned that our cellular system replenishes itself every four months.

Emotional well-being - Tahitian Noni Juice reduces your emotional reaction to stress and anxiety. It helps you feel better. Stress is a major cause of disease and possible cause of Multiple Sclerosis.

Tahitian Noni Juice helps the body but there are other things you need also do to assist the body. You need proper rest, exercise, vegetables, fruits, nuts and fresh air. You need to wear clothing made of natural fabrics.

In April 1998 I drove to Rockford, Illinois for a training event after working on a temporary assignment all week. In April 1999, I drove to

THE GIFT OF MULTIPLE SCLEROSIS

Gurnee, Illinois one Friday evening after working all week. I returned to Gurnee the following morning.

I accepted a full-time job after working as a temporary employee. I hosted satellite meetings for Tahitian Noni International and worked marketing events with my team. I was on fire!

I attended Tahitian Noni International conventions in Nashville, Tennessee, Anaheim, California and Salt Lake City, Utah with my TNI team.

My Nigerian mentor prepared me for the Tahitian Noni Juice opportunity. Tahitian Noni International's leaders exposed me to a residual income. They say "money does not grow on trees" they were wrong because Tahitian Noni grows on trees.

A Tahitian Noni International top income earner Ken Roland recommended the book "Rich Dad Poor Dad".

LINDA MOKEME

Linda in Anaheim, California at Morinda International event

THE GIFT OF MULTIPLE SCLEROSIS

Linda at Beverly Hills Hotel - 1999

I fell in love with an entrepreneur who had a business in my neighborhood. He was originally from Jamaica. I lost weight. Younger women felt they needed to compete with me. I consumed Tahitian Noni Juice daily.

Medical doctors had diagnosed me as having Multiple Sclerosis. Yet suddenly I was experiencing wellness. I did fifty jumping jacks a day. Tahitian Noni prepares the body for the "Gift" only God can give.

22

The ancient herb Hyssop and Tahitian Noni Juice brought me to the next level. Networking has taken me around the world, but Tahitian Noni Juice gave me the energy to enjoy the experience.

I began writing my autobiography before Tahitian Noni Juice. I thought I was finished when I started drinking Tahitian Noni Juice. Up to that point my life was extremely depressing. It was full of disappointment and loss.

Suddenly I was at peace. Consuming Hyssop and Tahitian Noni Juice I looked forward to being alive. "I have come that you may have life more abundantly."

Multiple Sclerosis – Tahitian Noni Juice regimen 1/3 to a ½ a bottle of a day, Whole bottle for 2 days bottle for a day.

Consume with your doctor's supervision. Inform your doctor you are drinking Tahitian Noni Juice.

Noni enhances the effectiveness of whatever else you are consuming i.e. blood pressure medicine...

Viruses cannot live in an oxygen enriched environment.

Do your own research. Good Health is an individual journey, just like a finger print.

Find out what works best for you.

Noni Instructions

Noni is best taken at your quieter times during the day—say maybe when you first get up or just before going to sleep at night.

Noni is an organic grape and blueberry juice. You may add some other juice to yours as you take it, if you do not like the taste. Do not add more than an ounce of another juice—you do not want to dilute it too much.

The regular dose is one ounce (two tablespoons) per day. If you have a medical problem, you may need more than that a day until condition is balanced.

Check with the person giving you your bottle about recommended amounts.

Make sure that you drink water. This will help to flush the toxins released by the Noni out of your systems. 6-8 glasses of water per day are recommended.

Recommended amounts of Noni – Check with your health professional for individual variances. The recommended daily dose is one ounce per day or two tablespoons. Each is best taken at quieter times during the day. Perhaps, each A.M. on arising or just before bedtimes.

If you have a health concern, one ounce, twice a day, is not too much.

Persons with inflammatory disorders or arthritis is suggested that you take one ounce, three (3), times a day for ten days, two weeks or less if the discomfort goes away before that time.

Terminally ill individuals with disorders such as cancer and the AIDS syndrome, may choose to take this once every four (4) of their waking hours.

When we first were introduced to Tahitian Noni Juice a Medical Physician Dr. Oliver Peale was a part of our upline's organization. He was based in Los Angeles, California.

He was a Director of a Hospice. Along with several wealthy distributors, he gifted Tahitian Noni Juice to his patients. The patients' improved. They did not die. They ended up closing the hospice facility.

23

In 1999, I purchased the book "Rich Dad Poor Dad" in a church bookstore. I immediately began reading it. "Rich Dad Poor Dad", is the brochure for the board game Cashflow.

In the year 2000, I rode in a Cadillac limousine with Michele the day of her daughter's funeral. Her daughter's memorial service was held in a funeral home in Chicago's Gold Coast. Famous Hollywood celebrities traveled to Chicago to attend the services. I stood at Michele's side as she begged the universe. "Please God do not let me leave my daughter in this grave yard".

In April 2001, I purchased the board game Cashflow at an Tahitian Noni International Convention in Salt Lake City, Utah. In April 2002, under the guidance of California medical doctor Dr. Oliver Peale and Natural physician Dr. Norman Rann, I switched to a vegan diet. They were both Tahitian Noni International distributors. They mentored our team on weekly Saturday morning conference calls. They taught us that eating animal products was detrimental to individuals with Cancer, Arthritis and Multiple Sclerosis.

LINDA MOKEME

To Michele,

"My beloved angel: When we met in 1995 I had no idea why the Universe had placed you in my life. Yet you filled the void that I struggled with for over 20 years. You are the good friend I always prayed for. Always know that you hold a very special place in my heart. I love you so very much. May the spirit of the living God give you peace in the loss of your beloved daughter Billie Neal.

Your friend,

Linda Mokeme

THE GIFT OF MULTIPLE SCLEROSIS

Celebrating my birthday at work -February 2002

24

Eliminating animal products from my diet transformed the quality of my life 360 degrees. Consuming animal products aggravate myelin sheets in the body which are already damaged in Multiple Sclerosis patients.

I went from being confined to my apartment to networking in the marketplace after working full-time. The vegan diet reduced the pain that I experienced on the left side of my body. Up until the day I became a vegan, I literally got on my own nerves.

The next month in May 2002, I was fired from my job. I was ten minutes late returning from lunch. It was payday and there was a long line at the currency exchange where I cashed my check. I only had time to purchase and eat my lunch.

I did not have time to go the bathroom. My supervisor was an African American male, Max. He was in his twenties. He told me I could not go to the bathroom. I responded saying I would go at my desk.

He wrote me up stating I said, "I would piss in the middle of the aisle". First, I am too much of a lady to ever express myself in that manner. In the past Max had let me know he did not think I had ever experienced stress.

THE GIFT OF MULTIPLE SCLEROSIS

Max and another African American male supervisor would perform Sambo dances for their managers. I had a hard time wrapping my brain around it. It was almost the 21st Century and there they were behaving like slaves.

Max called me into the conference room with his manager. They told me I was fired! The reason for my termination was "They did not like me". I jumped for joy! I quickly stood up and exited the meeting room.

I was focused on returning to my desk to get my belongings. That was not the reaction they were expecting. My supervisor called me back into the conference room. He told me it was mandatory I appeal their decision to terminate me. I was thankful to be terminated. I would take advantage of the opportunity and work with my friend Michele in her printing business. That afternoon I traveled to Aurora to attend my nephew Joshua's high school graduation.

My sister, Teresa drove me back to Chicago the following day. While we were on the expressway, I received a call from Michele's phone number. It was her nephew, Gary.

Michele had an asthma attack at a veterinarian clinic the day before. She had taken her dog for a checkup. She was pronounced D.O.A. (Dead on Arrival) at the hospital Emergency Room at 1PM. I was devastated!

Simultaneously, as I was being fired my best friend was dying. I was thankful to be away from my enemies at my job. I had the opportunity to grieve in private.

Michele and I were very close. I took her passing extremely hard. Michele had visited her daughter's gravesite for the first time since the day she was buried. Michele made her transition the next day. She died of a broken heart.

Following the advice of a friend, Brenda, an attorney I documented everything regarding my job situation. I was still very emotionally distraught on the day of my appointment with the Human Resources. After Human Resources read my appeal they immediately reinstated me to my job.

I let the H.R. manager know that my close friend had just passed away and I was in mourning. Human Resources scheduled my return to work after Michele's funeral services. By the day of Michele's funeral my left eye resembled "pink eye". I thought it was a result of my constant crying.

The managers at my job were livid when they read my appeal. From that point on they came after me with a vengeance. Simultaneously, Human Resources began an investigation into the department where I worked.

Still mourning Michele's passing I could not stop crying. My managers aggressively harassed me. They said I was weak because I was depressed because of my friend's passing. I did not care. I believed if I cried hard enough Michele would return to life just like Jesus.

The universe was good to me, therefore I felt that it would honor my request. Michele had buried her daughter Maureen, the year before and now she was gone.

Maureen lived her dream of being an actress. She lived in Beverly Hills, California. She was diagnosed as having a malignant brain tumor.

I experienced my left eye being inflamed. Everyone thought it was "pink eye". I made an appointment to see a medical doctor. It was not "pink eye".

THE GIFT OF MULTIPLE SCLEROSIS

In June 2002, I planned a vacation to Los Angeles. My managers gave me a difficult time, but I had earned vacation days. I had a right to take a vacation. A friend of mine, Susan who lived in Atlanta met me in Los Angeles. We stayed at the home of my entrepreneur friend, Mr. Sawyer in Hollywood, California.

By the end of August 2002 my employment environment was extremely toxic. Human Resources offered me the opportunity to leave the company with a small stipend. They requested I sign an agreement stating I would not sue them. At the time I was a mentee of Robert Kiyosaki, author of "Rich Dad Poor Dad".

Robert Kiyosaki's mentorship gave me the confidence to quick my job. I had the protection of the Human Resource department. Over Labor Day weekend, I made the decision to take advantage of the Human Resources offer. I turned in my resignation the day after Labor Day. I scheduled my last day at work for September 12, 2002.

LINDA MOKEME

*Linda in Hollywood,
California - June 2002*

Linda – 2003 Vegan diet

25

In July 2003, I persuaded four female friends to commit to play the board game Cashflow once a month for a year. Our group consisted of five women, a CPA/Attorney -Louise, a Chicago Public School teacher -Bernice, a Flight Attendant/Entrepreneur- Dora, a Sales Executive- Terry and myself.

I had a friend, Lisa who was working in a law office. The attorney, Bonita needed legal documents typed. Lisa only had experience working as a professional model. She could not type. She called me consistently from August through September begging me to come and work with them at the law office.

She wanted me to be their typist. I was not interested. Finally, I recognized it was an opportunity. In September, I interviewed with the Attorney Bonita. She offered to pay me $10 per hour. I was insulted, yet I remembered Rich Dad taught that the rich do not work for money. They work to learn. I accepted the job as an Independent Contractor.

Shortly afterwards I discovered the law office did not have heat in the winter. Déjà vu, I had lived in a studio apartment for eight years without any heat. It was my experience when I first returned from Nigeria.

THE GIFT OF MULTIPLE SCLEROSIS

On Sunday, December 7, I was getting dressed for church when I received the telephone call from Michigan. My dad had made his transition that morning. I continued getting dressed because my ride was scheduled to pick me within the hour. I cried all the way to church and throughout church services.

My dad had purchased five new suits the day before. Three suits were still at the men's store. They needed to be tailored.

I worked up until the day of my dad's funeral. I did not get paid for time off from work. I rode with my brother-in-law to be with my family. My other siblings had been in Michigan all week.

Immediately after the funeral services my step siblings became were antagonistic. My stepbrother's wife wanted to sleep with me.

I chose to sleep on the couch in the family room. My step-mother was sleeping on the opposite couch in the family room as well. My step siblings thought I was sleeping near my step-mother to watch her financial moves.

It was a nightmare! The next day my step-siblings were extremely abusive. They were territorial and threw my siblings and I out of my dad's house that night. That ended my grieving period. I blamed my dad!

I was thankful I was playing the board game Cashflow. Robert Kiyosaki guaranteed playing the board game for one year would improve your life financially. I trusted him. Whenever I followed his advice "magic" happened.

In January 2004, Dr. Townsend volunteered to help me with my Tahitian Noni business. He was traveling to Nigeria in February. He committed to help me with my network there. I had lunch with him and his sister, Diane the day of his international flight, February 13.

I gave him marketing materials and Tahitian Noni research information to give to my Nigerian Tahitian Noni network. He had a massive heart attack, three days after he arrived in Nigeria. It happened on Mom's birthday, February 16. He was in a coma until he made his transition on February 22. I attended his funeral on my 14th leap year birthday, February 29, 2004!

In April 2004, Lisa quit working at the law office. She was livid because the attorney did not share the profits she received from a million-dollar law suit. The attorney had recently reached a settlement.

Lisa wanted me to quit along with her. I was not financially able to quit. I had bills to pay. The

Attorney, Bonita, gave me a check for $1000.00 the day Lisa quit. She needed me to stay. I had no choice!

An attorney, Laverne, who I had been my close friend for over 20 years recommended a friend of her daughter's, Vanessa to work with us in the law office. Attorney, Bonita hired Vanessa and we soon learned Vanessa was a serious "thug".

Vanessa antagonized me and a young African American female attorney, who had an office in our large suite. After an extremely toxic environment the attorney fired Vanessa in August. My friend, Laverne accused me of being responsible for Vanessa being terminated. Laverne and I have never spoken again.

THE GIFT OF MULTIPLE SCLEROSIS

In October 2004, I received a letter addressed to me at the law office. It was in a red, white and blue envelope. There was something compelling about the letter. It was postmarked from Nevada. It was from the Neo-Tech Society.

I was extremely vulnerable. For several years, I pleaded with the universe for help. Through Rich

Dad I was aware that we were in the Information Age. I discerned that Neo-Tech's product was information. Therefore, I went for it. I started manifesting instantly.

I did integrated thinking and got the heat turned on in the law office. I finally received a return on my Nigerian investments. I acquired a designer wardrobe. I went from a size 16 to size 12 dress size. I stopped wearing wigs. I learned to be proud of my natural hair.

LINDA MOKEME

Linda in Evanston marketplace July 2005 wearing a wig.

THE GIFT OF MULTIPLE SCLEROSIS

2005 – The first year of my Neothink journey

LINDA MOKEME

Linda wearing her natural hair - 2006

THE GIFT OF MULTIPLE SCLEROSIS

By July 2005, it was time for me to go to the next level regarding playing the board game Cashflow. Most of our players had quit. I saw an ad in the newspaper regarding a Cashflow 202 group in the Chicago area. I telephoned the coordinator.

Their games were hosted in the Northwest suburbs in private residences. My desire to go to the next level motivated me to take public transportation to remote suburban locations. As usual, I experienced racism from the white hosts.

One Sunday, a Cashflow host who had just returned from church services objected to my presence in his Des Plaines apartment. I was the only guest he insulted. I persevered despite the racism I encountered until I was confident I knew the fundamentals of playing the game. Finally, I was ready to play Cashflow 202 with my Chicago Public School teacher friend, Bonita.

In October 2005, I attended a weekend seminar where Robert Kiyosaki was one of the main speakers. He let us know the dollar was now fiat money. He encouraged us to "Fail, Forward, Fast!". I returned to the law office the following Monday focused on leaving.

I answered an ad in a free local newspaper. It was placed by a financial services company. They scammed me out of my rent money. The attorney, Bonita overheard me on the phone asking my brother-in-law for a $500 loan.

She volunteered to lend me $500. When I was unable to repay her back by the next pay check she started treating me like her slave. She made me work the entire day on Christmas Eve.

The first week of January 2006 she terminated me. She was angry because I found out she was being evicted from the law office. She refused to pay the electric bill in the law office for several years. After she failed to inform her landlord there was a flood in our suite he terminated her lease.

I accepted a temporary assignment in March 2006 to work at Catholic Charities. I worked at

Catholic Charities faithfully until my assignment ended in January 2007.

On February 16, 2007, I received the book "Miss Annabelle's Secrets" in the mail. It was written by Mark Hamilton. I have never looked back. By April 2007, Mark Hamilton, invited individuals to be his "Apprentice" for one year. I took advantage of the opportunity. At the time "The Apprentice" was the only program I watched on television.

In April 2007, I re-entered the traditional medical system because my left eye was inflamed. It looked like a spider web. The doctors administered a series of tests. They ruled out "pink eye". They prescribed eye medication because they could see an inflammation was crippling my eye. They did not know what it was, but they were confident it was not Multiple Sclerosis.

The prescription eye drops made me lethargic. It caused me to be terminated from a temporary assignment. At the same time, I was experiencing multiple physical challenges due to stress.

THE GIFT OF MULTIPLE SCLEROSIS

I was wearing dark sunglasses because my left eye was crippled.

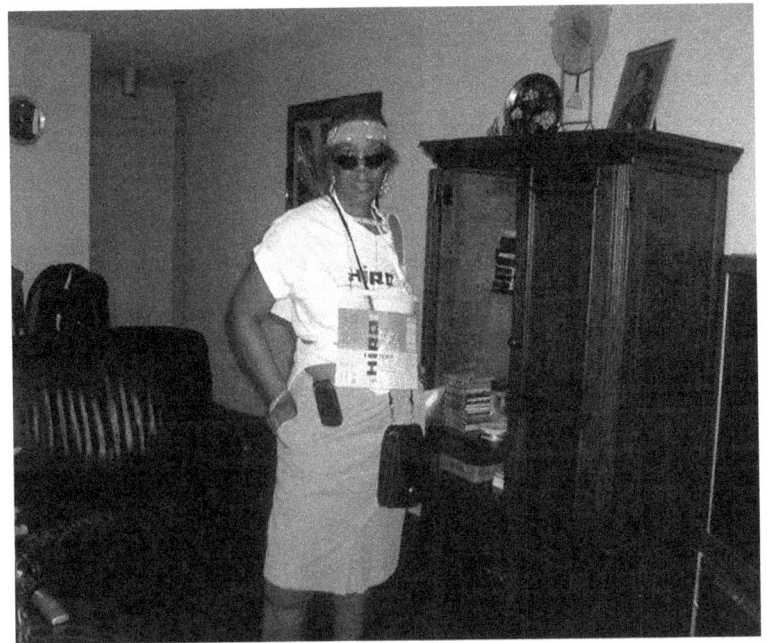

26

In June 2007, I rented a car and drove to Rockford, Illinois to attend my first Neothink Clubhouse Meeting. I was unemployed. I used my link card to buy food as my contribution to the event. I was the only black individual there. It was hosted in a Neothink members apartment.

During the introductions I learned a few attendees also lived in the Chicago area. The Chicago residents scheduled a meetup in Chicago for July. As always, I experienced racism. They recommended that I start a separate group for Neothink Clubhouse Meetings. I continued attending their meetings.

Mark Hamilton's right-hand man reached out to me in August 2007. I was the Neothink Society's Chicago point of contact. I was elated but the other Chicago Neothink members were livid. They resented a black female being their Neothink Clubhouse point of contact.

In August 2007, I accepted an indefinite temporary assignment at a Medical Health Clinic. I was the receptionist. It was the perfect job for me because I read my Neothink Manuscripts all day. I also telephoned other members while I was at work.

THE GIFT OF MULTIPLE SCLEROSIS

In January 2008, members of our Neothink Clubhouse team scheduled an emergency meeting. Their mission was to psychologically lynch me. They did not want me on their team.

When their attack failed three of the members quit in March 2008. An Italian male and an Black male were the only ones who remained. The Italian male's goal was to sabotage the success of my clubhouse.

In June 2008, he told me he could not imagine Queen Elizabeth putting a black person in a leadership position. He consistently verbally attacked me. In the beginning of August 2008, we had our final confrontation. Ironically, Barack Obama won the Democratic nomination for the President of the United States that same month.

At the end of August 2008, my brother was diagnosed with Stage IV Lung Cancer. The Italian member submitted his resignation at our September Neothink Clubhouse Meeting.

One of the physicians at the medical clinic did not like me. He was from Bulgaria. He aggressively worked to get me removed from the assignment. I experienced jealously from one of his patients who was a black female. The stress caused me to lose mobility in my right thumb.

On Friday, October 17, I visited my brother, Emerson at Rush Presbyterian St. Luke hospital after I got off work. He was on life support. He had a broken expression on his face.

His doctors showed us an X-ray of his Lungs. His lungs were blackened! Half of one lung was missing and the other was very deteriorated. That day at work I had experienced excessive stress from the Bulgarian doctor. It was a very dark day!

LINDA MOKEME

Attending the African Festival Arts that Labor Day weekend helped me feel better during that extremely challenging moment.

THE GIFT OF MULTIPLE SCLEROSIS

That night, I experienced a deep depression. The next day I attended a memorial service of a friend's mother-in-law. As I attended the services my family made the decision to remove my brother from life support. He made his transition instantly.

I received a call after work hours the next business day. It was my temporary agency supervisor. The Bulgarian physician requested I be replaced. I slipped into a deep depression. It lasted for weeks. For the first time in weeks I woke up on Tuesday, November 4, 2008 "Feeling good"! The sun was shining brightly into my studio apartment. I started dancing! History was made that evening. Barack Obama won the presidential election.

From the moment Barack Obama won the election I experienced special treatment. The bus I boarded near Union Station drove me all the way to my neighborhood. Normally I would need to transfer to a different bus. The driver said it was a result of the request of our new President.

On November 6, 2008 I was at the Daley Center standing outside a courtroom. The prosecuting assistant, a black woman asked me how I ended up being summoned to court regarding delinquent credit payments. With tears in my eyes I replied that people did not like me. With compassion she responded, "They did not like Jesus Christ either".

LINDA MOKEME

On my way to my brother's funeral services - October 25, 2008.

27

I was still unemployed in February 2009 when the Neothink Society introduced its members to the CD set "Your Wish Is Your Command". Members were excited about the letter they received in the mail introducing them to the "Your Wish Is Your Command" CDs.

I had not received the letter. It did not bother me because I did not have $300 which was the cost to purchase the CDs. For my birthday February 28, a member on our National Neothink Health and Wellness team gifted me a copy of the CD set. I listened to "Your Wish Is Your Command" repeatedly. The magic began. I cultivated a desire to join the Global Information Network but did not know how I would pay for it.

I could barely pay my rent. I received minimum unemployment benefits. Listening to the CD set "Your Wish Is Your Command" I wanted to become a member, but I did not have $1000 dollars to pay the initiation fee.

LINDA MOKEME

Linda making a presentation at Neothink Clubhouse Meeting – April 2009

During the month of March 2009 President Barack Obama gave individuals who were on unemployment a $100.00 monthly stipend.

In June 2009 a new Neothink member, Timothy reached out to me. He lived in Champaign-Urbana. He was a white male who was a Christian. He wanted to know if Neothink members believed in God. We talked by phone daily. He let me know he had once been an extremely successful businessman. His business had failed because of the economic crisis. His driver's license was revoked due to multiple DUI's he had acquired.

THE GIFT OF MULTIPLE SCLEROSIS

He described the comfortable lifestyle he had. He lived in Champaign with his wife. She was an executive at the University of Illinois. We shared our individual experiences. I confided in him that I was experiencing a challenge with roaches in my apartment. I did not have enough money to buy roach spray.

On July 18, 2009, I met Infomercial King Kevin Trudeau and his wife Natasha at an International

Neothink/TVP Convention. The convention was held at the Hyatt Regency in Rosemont, Illinois. The day that we met Kevin Trudeau, he offered our group a payment plan option to become a member of the Global Information Network.

We could join his organization Natural Cures as a Lifetime member and our GIN initiation fee would be waived. The cost of becoming a Lifetime member of Natural Cures was $1500. We had the option of paying $100 a month for 15 months. In fully integrated honesty I was still hesitant regarding taking advantage of Kevin's opportunity.

I shared the opportunity with the Neothink member in Champaign, IL. He marked the last day of the window of opportunity on his calendar. On the last day July 31, 2009, he took advantage of Kevin's opportunity. He signed up in my affiliate organization because he wanted to help me be successful.

By 8PM as the window of opportunity was ending, I realized I was the minister on top of the roof and a flood was coming. What if this was my life boat? I took a leap of faith and took advantage of Kevin Trudeau's opportunity. I used my unemployment $100 monthly stipend to pay for the Natural Cures Lifetime membership.

In August 2009, the Global Information Network held their first Member's Only meeting at the Drake Hotel in Chicago. Members of the Neothink Society from around the country would be in Chicago to attend the Members-only meeting. I could not let Neothink members come to Chicago and not be with them.

On August 9, I upgraded my GIN status from Affiliate to Member. My luck changed instantly for the good. Up to that moment I had struggled playing the board game Cashflow for six years. From the moment I joined the Global Information Network I became lucky playing the game. I did not know what I did not know but I knew the only difference was I was a member of the Global Information Network.

In September 2009, the white male GIN member who lived in Champaign told me he felt sorry for me. He joined my team to help me be successful. From the moment he joined my team certain employees at GIN's administrative office gave him an extremely hard time. Being a black female, I was accustomed to being given a hard time.

I talked to Timothy on the phone the day after Labor Day! He was livid! He had been on the phone with GIN Support all weekend regarding the $1000 initiation fee they had deducted from his account. He stopped payment on the $1000 which reversed his GIN status to Affiliate.

They had deducted the $1000 from my checking account as well. I brought my situation to Kevin Trudeau's attention at the August Members-only meeting. Kevin asked me if I had signed up any members. When I told him, I had signed up three members he immediately instructed his staff to redeposit the $1000 back into my account.

THE GIFT OF MULTIPLE SCLEROSIS

Captured during the summer of 2009 at State & Roosevelt in Chicago

Timothy's communications with the GIN support team made him extremely negative. He was angry with Kevin Trudeau and Mark Hamilton. He wanted me to contact them on his behalf. I felt it was not my issue.

I stopped communicating with him even though he made it clear that he was not angry with me. I did not hear from him for three weeks. When I was unable to contact him by phone decided to look him up on Facebook. I discovered he was in a fatal bike accident, three days after our last conversation.

LINDA MOKEME

Attending Teresa's 50th Birthday party November 1, 2009 – Green Dolphin Club, Chicago

THE GIFT OF MULTIPLE SCLEROSIS

Playing the board game Cashflow 202

"It is not what you have it is who you become!"

28

By October 2009, I did not have enough money to pay my rent. An African American Neothink couple advised me to contact my landlord to negotiate a payment plan.

By this time, I had lost the use of both thumbs. I could not bend either one of them. If they did bend they were stuck in the bent position. I suffered with that health issue for over a year. Through the Global Information Network, I learned about Vitamin D3. Consuming Vitamin D3 restored both thumbs to normalcy.

On Saturday, December 26, 2009 walking to the bus as I carried two heavy grocery bags I slipped and fell on the icy snow. It happened in a cleaners parking lot in Skokie. I fractured my left ankle in two places. The same attorney friend Laura who told me to document everything regarding my employment recommended a Jewish personal injury lawyer. He was her first employer. I called him on Monday, December 28 and he immediately took me on as his client pro bono. I did not have any medical insurance. He referred me to chiropractor who treated me without insurance.

LINDA MOKEME

*Linda at Olympics Event – Chicago celebration, October 2, 2009
Holding the Olympic Torch*

Linda at GIN Event April 10, 2010 – Sheraton, Louisville, KY

THE GIFT OF MULTIPLE SCLEROSIS

My fractured ankle complicated challenges I was already experiencing on the left side of my body. Stress was having crippling effects on various parts of my body. I experienced inflammations which crippled my left eye on multiple occasions.

On Saturday, October 16, 2010 I attended a GIN Members only event in Rosemont, Illinois. The speaker was so focused on sharing the information he had acquired he did not stop to give us breaks. That evening I was unable to walk. I was in an extremely vulnerable position.

On Monday, October 18, 2010, my Jewish attorney called me. He asked me to come to his office. When I arrived in his office. He told me someone upstairs likes you. The insurance company had offered me a settlement. It occurred the same month that my unemployment ended permanently.

In April 2011, I re-entered the medical system because of my double fractured left ankle. The intake physician immediately diagnosed me with depression and schizophrenia.

The neurologist assigned to my case rejected the idea that I had Multiple Sclerosis. He said I was insane if I thought that I had MS. He said I should see a psychiatrist.

He scheduled me for EMG tests. I was confident that the results would show the excruciating pain I was experiencing. My tests results were normal. I thought if the pain I was experiencing in my back was normal then I had to be insane.

In June 2011, I met a minister who was visiting Chicago. He lived in Nigeria. He was a powerful and influential billionaire. He was in Chicago to check on two of his mentees. They were a married couple.

He wanted to confirm that their ministry had not been corrupted by the American culture. He was the guest speaker the day I met him. His presentation was about marriage.

After service I approached him and privately shared my marriage experience. He said I had two choices: 1) reunite with my ex-husband or 2) let God be my husband. I chose the latter. The minister made his transition a few weeks later.

In December 2011, my neurologist scheduled me for an MRI. My appointment was on December 21 at 10 in the morning. I waited seven hours in the basement of John Stroger's Hospital for the MRI technicians to arrive to administer the MRI. The next month January 2012 when I arrived for my follow-up appointment I learned my neurologist was hospitalized that day. They rescheduled my appointment for April 3, 2012.

On April 3, 2012 an intern physician came into the patient's room to talk to me. He told me my results were positive revealing an advanced stage of Multiple Sclerosis. I broke down crying! My neurologist came into the room. He was dumbfounded. How could an individual live with MS for twenty-seven years without medical attention.

THE GIFT OF MULTIPLE SCLEROSIS

Visiting a friend November 13, 2010 in Bolingbrook, IL on my way to a GIN event in Oakbrook, IL

LINDA MOKEME

Attending a GIN event
December 15, 2010
Marriott Chicago O'Hare

THE GIFT OF MULTIPLE SCLEROSIS

My first Caribbean cruise GIN event January 28-30, 2011

LINDA MOKEME

In our cabin room during GIN Caribbean cruise January 28-30, 2011

Visiting family in Tennessee

At GIN Caribbean Cruise – Platinum Event
January 19, 2012

My neurologist said I made him a "believer". From that point on he respected my health and wellness choices. All those years of suffering and reaching out for help with no success was all too much. I broke down crying.

After my doctor's appointment, I was thankful and grateful I was affiliated with Kevin Trudeau because I had access to a network of Health & Wellness professionals. Luckily, I had a Local Chapter Meeting in Oakbrook, Illinois that evening.

During a follow-up medical visit my neurologist told me I had benign Multiple Sclerosis. His assessment of my MS experience let me know he did not have a clue!

THE GIFT OF MULTIPLE SCLEROSIS

April 3, 2012 - The day my Neurologist confirmed my MRI tests results were positive for Multiple Sclerosis

LINDA MOKEME

Art Institute of Chicago - 2012

29

I upgraded from Tahitian Noni Juice to TruAge Max in June 2012. Drinking TruAge Max gave me the energy I needed for my new fast paced lifestyle. In July 2012, I attended a seminar with the guest speaker Montel Vial, PhD. The event was a National Neothink convention held at Chicago's McCormick Place.

I was aware Montel Vial's promoted a diet that required the elimination of some fruits and vegetables. Being on a vegan diet, I was not interested in attending his seminar.

There I was on Sunday, July 22, 2012 attending Montel Vial's seminar. He was extremely persuasive. He introduced us to the value of Qi. I immediately applied what I learned. I had no choice! I had Multiple Sclerosis!

In October 2012, I attended a GIN Family Reunion in Nashville, Tennessee. I had high expectations but never in my wildest dreams did I expect what I experienced. The first day of the event I met a Qi Grand Master. He was a VIP guest at our GIN Platinum meeting.

The next day the Grand Master invited several GIN members including my sister and I to his room to experience his Qi (Chi) demonstrations.

LINDA MOKEME

Each attendee experienced and witnessed the amazing power of Qi (Chi). It was powerful! I remained in the background attempting to hide my disability. When the turn came for my Qi experience I was terrified of falling. I let the Grand Master know I had Multiple Sclerosis. He told me a Qi Cleansings would help me.

Linda at GIN Platinum Event in Chicago – June 21, 2012

THE GIFT OF MULTIPLE SCLEROSIS

Linda at GIN Platinum event – October 18, 2012 in B.B. King's in Nashville, Tennessee

"If you want to live to be 100. Do Qi Gong!" - Dr. Oz

The Grand Master transferred his Qi energy into my body. After my Qi experience my sister noticed I was walking faster. The next day I volunteered to drive back to Chicago from Nashville. I did not have energy to help drive from Chicago to Nashville. I experienced an amazing energy that lasted for over a week.

LINDA MOKEME

International Gem Show –
December 8, 2012

THE GIFT OF MULTIPLE SCLEROSIS

I did not know what I did not know but I had a powerful Qi (Chi) energy after being activated by the Grand Master. Although I had physical limitations I took advantage of every opportunity to experience the Grand Master's workshop events.

I had so much energy it was overwhelming. I saw the Grand Master again in Miami, Florida. It was January 2013. I was returning from a cruise to the Bahamas as the Grand Master arrived for a cruise to Mexico. I needed another Qi treatment.

In February 2013, the Grand Master held a Martial Artists event in Chicago. I had the extraordinary opportunity to attend and discover how highly respected he was in the Chicago Martial Arts community. It was extremely impressive! Limited by Multiple Sclerosis I attended one of his Qi Gong trainings. I captured the experience on video as I sat in the background.

By the time I saw the Grand Master in Dallas, Texas during a GIN convention in April 2013, I was begging for his Qi treatment. The weather difference between Dallas and Chicago weakened my immune system. I was immediately challenged with the flu when I returned home. After I recovered my energy level was extremely low. After struggling with Multiple Sclerosis twenty-eight years I believed the end was near.

By June 2013, I was desperate to improve my health status, so I began rebounding. I experienced an immediate surge of energy and communicated my experience to the Grand Master who was living in Hot Springs, Arkansas.

LINDA MOKEME

When I learned the Grand Master was having a Qi Gong event in the Chicago area I signed up to attend.. During the weekend of July 2013, I participated in my first Qi Gong seminar. I participated in my second Qi Gong seminar during the weekend of August 2013. That month I was like an ever-ready battery.

Labor Day Weekend 2013, I experienced a stressful situation which caused a painful relapse. I was in excruciating pain. I wished the Grand Master was in Chicago. Fortunately, the Grand

Master and his team were in town because I had the opportunity to experience my first Qi (Chi) Cleansing. It worked magically! I went from being in crippling pain to doing "the Twist" when they completed the treatment an hour later.

In October 2013, after returning from a GIN Family Reunion in Washington, DC I had another painful relapse. Thank goodness, the Grand Master was still in town because I experienced my second Qi (Chi) Cleansing. I recovered instantly from a crippling pain.

From October 2013 through February 2017, I attended Qi Gong training at least two days a week. I learned to cultivate my Qi (Chi) as instructed by The Grand Master.

When the Grand Master and his Qi Gong team relocated to Chicago I never missed a class. I traveled two hours each way on public transportation through heavy snow storms and below zero weather. The Grand Master and his team often gave me a ride home.

For decades, I barely existed because I was always in pain. Thanks to the powerful Qi Gong training I am pain free and have rejuvenated my youthful zeal.

In early 2015 my neurologist released me as his patient. He said whatever I was doing to keep it up because it was working. He recommended I get a Physical Care Physician (PCP) regarding the maintenance of my overall health care.

I was pleased with the value of Qi Gong, but I continued to experience challenges on the left side of my body. In October 2016, I attended a MS seminar where the neurologist explained that spinal & nerve issues never heal.

LINDA MOKEME

Linda at Hair Salon – January 2013

THE GIFT OF MULTIPLE SCLEROSIS

*Linda at Union Pizzeria Celebrating my birthday
with friends February 23, 2013
— Evanston, Illinois*

LINDA MOKEME

*Linda with her grandnephew, Jaeden Dominic –
RIP March 8, 2011 – January 28, 2015*

THE GIFT OF MULTIPLE SCLEROSIS

Celebrating my birthday at Bank of America Theatre
— February 28, 2013
— The Book of Mormon

LINDA MOKEME

At GIN Event – Go 5 Star – June 8, 2013
– Hyatt Regency O'Hare

THE GIFT OF MULTIPLE SCLEROSIS

First Look for Charity – Chicago Auto Show at McCormick Place – Friday, February 7, 2014

LINDA MOKEME

Linda at Kevin Trudeau's Contempt of Court sentencing –

Dirksen Federal Building

Monday, March 17, 2014 -

THE GIFT OF MULTIPLE SCLEROSIS

Linda at Earth, Wind & Fire Concert – July 3, 2014
Ravinia Festival Park, Highland Park, Illinois

LINDA MOKEME

Linda at Networking Event – Des Plaines, IL – October 2014

At Martial Arts facility - October 2014

THE GIFT OF MULTIPLE SCLEROSIS

Linda at the "Theory of Everything" – Evanston Theaters, November 2014

LINDA MOKEME

Linda at Jaeden Dominic's memorial – Saturday. March 7, 2015 Dempsey's Marriott Midway

THE GIFT OF MULTIPLE SCLEROSIS

Linda – April 2015

LINDA MOKEME

Celebrating my sisters' birthday – Sunday, November 8, 2015

Linda hosting Neothink Clubhouse Meeting – Sunday, October 16, 016

THE GIFT OF MULTIPLE SCLEROSIS

Renowned international naturopathic physician Dr. Finley was so impressed with Tahitian Noni Juice that she was planning to replace her entire inventory with Tahitian Noni Juice. Your skin is the largest organ. It is a great receptor for Noni.

In October 2016, I attended a MS seminar where I learned from the neurologist speaker that nerve damage is irreversible.

In 2016 Morinda, Inc added Tahitian Noni Essential Oils to their product line. In October, I began using the Tahitian Noni Essential Oil Recover Blend. Finally, I have iron grip control regarding the left side of my body. Tahitian Noni Essential Oil Recover Blend is the missing puzzle piece regarding controlling my nerve pain. I massage it into my lower back area and my left thigh to just below my knee. It has a pleasant aroma. It is soothing and relaxing. I took advantage of a Morinda International promotion and ordered 3 Tahitian Noni Essential Oils and Morinda gifted me with a diffuser.

And by the river upon the bank thereof, on this side and on that side, shall grow all trees for meat, whose leaf shall not fade, neither shall the fruit thereof be consumed: it shall bring forth new fruit according to his months, because their waters they issued out of the sanctuary, and the fruit thereof shall be for meat, and the leaf thereof for medicine." Ezekiel 47:12

LINDA MOKEME

Linda at Chicago Urban League Golden Fellowship Dinner – Chicago Hilton November 19, 2016

THE GIFT OF MULTIPLE SCLEROSIS

Linda at MS Event – Wildfire Steaks, Chops & Seafood – Thursday, December 1, 2016

LINDA MOKEME

Visiting my sister Shirley on Friday, December 9, 2016

THE GIFT OF MULTIPLE SCLEROSIS

*Linda at Neothink Clubhouse Meeting
– Sunday, March 15, 2017*

LINDA MOKEME

I woke up on Tuesday March 28, 2017 feeling a bit discombobulated. I had just researched the status of my friend Debbie's mentor, Deborah, who also had Multiple Sclerosis. Our common denominators were uncanny. Deborah worked at AT&T in a management capacity. I worked my way up through the ranks at AT&T before I moved to Nigeria 20 years later.

Both Deborah and I were extremely giving regarding our friend Debbie's trajectory. Deborah was diagnosed with MS decades ago. I was diagnosed with MS three decades ago. Deborah made her transition in 2003. I began playing the board game Cashflow in 2003 which transformed my journey. Deborah was only one year older than me.

Ravinia Festival – Stevie Nicks, September 9, 2017

THE GIFT OF MULTIPLE SCLEROSIS

Ravinia Festival – Boz Scaggs - June 27, 2017

Ravinia Festival – Carlos Santana, August 12, 2017

LINDA MOKEME

Ravinia Festival - Stevie Nicks, September 9, 2017

Ravinia Festival – September 15, 2017, Smokey Robinson

AFTERWORD

I began reading Neothink Multigenerational Manuscripts in December 2004. In 2006 I filed for my international divorce and it was final in February 2007. In February 2007 I read the book Miss Annabelle's Secrets. In June 2007, I committed to an apprenticeship program with the founder of the Neothink Society, Mark Hamilton. I have coordinated Neothink Clubhouse Meetings in the Chicago area since October 2007. That Area of Responsibility has empowered me with the Neothink Mentality. In 2008, I went to the next level and volunteered to be a part the National Neothink Health and Wellness team.

The information in the Neothink Prime Literature is priceless.

The Prime Literature is the foundation of our Neothink Society local chapters.

Our mission is to make everyone wealthy, including the poor.

The goal of the Neothink Society is help individuals live the life they are meant to live minus the dishonesty. The Neothink Prime Literature contains information which gives you enormous advantages. You become smarter than a Harvard graduate.

What if everything you needed to know to have everything you always wanted was written somewhere? For the first-time ever, everything you need to know to win in every area of your life is now available within the Neothink Society. Applying the information that I learned I finally earned income from my network in Nigeria.

LINDA MOKEME

I used Neothink techniques to get my international divorce. I was separated from my husband over 13 years. My Neothink journey has given me iron-grip control in every area of my life.

The Neothink Society - Twelve Visions World

Vision Three

…The geniuses eradicate disease after disease and drive down medical costs. People live with nearly perfect health, well into their hundreds, or longer…

The value of being a member of the Neothink Society is priceless. How apropos that during the Information Age our product is information. When the Neothink Society reached out to me I was at the lowest point of my life. Their marketing material promised to help me, and they delivered.

Integrating with other Neothink members I was aware Health and Wellness continued to be my priority. Meeting the author of the book "Natural Cures "They" Don't Want You to Know About" Kevin Trudeau at a Neothink convention was a life changing experience. I had seen Kevin's infomercials. I agreed with the information he shared. My Health and Wellness journey taught me "You Don't Have to Be Sick!" I learned sickness and disease is "big business". Follow the trail of the money!

Find your "Why"!

I suffered physically, emotionally, mentally and financially for decades. From the beginning of my Multiple Sclerosis diagnosis I was aware of

THE GIFT OF MULTIPLE SCLEROSIS

my physical limitations. I was aware that I could not work a job and maintain an intimate relationship.

In January 1994, I moved to Nigeria to live with my husband whom I married in June 1993. By the time I joined the Neothink Society in the fall of 2004 I was begging the universe for help. The first day that I met Kevin Trudeau he offered our group a hand-up.

In fully integrated honesty, I was skeptical. I did not immediately take advantage of Kevin's offer. As the window of opportunity was closing, I faced the fact I was drowning. What if this was my life boat? I decided to take a leap of faith and joined the Global Information Network. My life changed for the good. The wisdom and guidance I received from Kevin helped me get back on my feet. Through Kevin I met a mentor who has effectively helped me overcome the painful challenges of Multiple Sclerosis.

I did not know what I did not know but I was aware as a member of the Global Information Network I had access to a network of natural physicians.

Living with the pain of Multiple Sclerosis was unbearable. Struggling to keep a roof over my head. I lived with the embarrassing secret that I was unable to hold the water in my bladder. Having MS made me insecure. I was always conscious of my back issues. I felt extremely vulnerable because anything could cripple me. Multiple Sclerosis is a full-time experience. I coped by remaining silent. There were days I got on my own nerves.

13 *Though I speak with the tongues of men and of angels, but have not love, I have become sounding brass or a clanging cymbal.* ²*And though I have the gift of prophecy, and understand all mysteries and all knowledge, and though I have all faith, so that I could remove*

- *mountains, but have not love, I am nothing.* ³*And though I bestow all my goods to feed the poor, and though I give my body to be burned,[a] but have not love, it profits me nothing.*

- ⁴*Love suffers long and is kind; love does not envy; love does not parade itself, is not puffed up;* ⁵*does not behave rudely, does not seek its own, is not provoked, thinks no evil;* 6*does not rejoice in iniquity, but rejoices in the truth;* 7*bears all things, believes all things, hopes all things, endures all things.*

- ⁸*Love never fails. But whether there are prophecies, they will fail; whether there are tongues, they will cease; whether there is knowledge, it will vanish away.* 9*For we know in part and we prophesy in part.* 10*But when that which is perfect has come, then that which is in part will be done away.*

- ¹¹*When I was a child, I spoke as a child, I understood as a child, I thought as a child; but when I became a man, I put away childish things.* ¹²*For now we see in a mirror, dimly, but then face to face.*

- *Now I know in part, but then I shall know just as I also am known.*

- ¹³*And now abide faith, hope, love, these three; but the greatest of these is love.*

ENDNOTES

- Multiple Sclerosis is thought to affect more than 2.3 million people worldwide. While the disease is not contagious or directly inherited, epidemiologists — scientists who study patterns of disease — have identified factors in the distribution of MS around the world that may eventually help determine what causes the disease. These factors include <u>gender</u>, genetics, age, geography and ethnic background.

- **Epidemiology** is the branch of medicine that deals with the incidence, distribution, and possible control of diseases and other factors relating to health. Epidemiological studies are challenging for several reasons:

- MS can be difficult to diagnose. Since there is no single test for MS, the diagnosis can be missed, delayed or even incorrect.

- MS is not a "reportable" disease, which means that the government does not require physicians to inform any central database when they make the diagnosis. Without this kind of centralized reporting system, there is no easy way to count people with MS.

- Data from earlier epidemiological studies may not accurately represent the current MS population because the investigators used different methods for identifying and counting people with MS, as well as different strategies for analyzing their data.

- Therefore, all epidemiological numbers are estimates.

Incidence and prevalence

- The **incidence** of a disease is the number of new cases occurring in a given period of time (usually a year) in a given population (usually 100,000). With the challenges inherent in promptly and correctly identifying people with MS, arriving at an accurate incidence figure has been virtually impossible.

- The **prevalence** of MS is the number of people with MS at a particular point in time, in a particular place. Most epidemiological studies in MS focus on prevalence.

- While prevalence is a bit easier to determine than incidence, the diagnostic issues can distort these figures as well, since all persons with MS are included in prevalence figures regardless of how long they have had the disease. Of the MS prevalence studies that have been conducted worldwide, the data from the northern hemisphere are the most reliable thus far. The Society is working to improve reporting.

Epidemiological estimates

- Although more people are being diagnosed with MS today than in the past, the reasons for this are not clear. Likely contributors, however, include greater awareness of the disease, better access to medical care and improved diagnostic capabilities. There is no definitive evidence that the rate of MS is generally on the increase.

- **Age:** Most people are diagnosed between the ages of 20 and 50, although MS can occur in young children and significantly older adults.

THE GIFT OF MULTIPLE SCLEROSIS

- **Geography:** In general, MS is more common in areas farthest from the equator. However, prevalence rates may differ significantly among groups living in the same geographic area regardless of distance from the equator. For example, in spite of the latitude at which they live, MS is almost unheard of in some populations, including the Inuit, Yakutes, Hutterites, Hungarian Romani, Norwegian Lapps, Australian Aborigines and New Zealanders — indicating that ethnicity and geography interact in some complex way to impact prevalence figures in different parts of the world. Migration from one geographic area to another seems to alter a person's risk of developing MS. Studies indicate that immigrants and their descendants tend to take on the risk level — either higher or lower — of the area to which they move. The change in risk, however, may not appear immediately. Those who move in early childhood tend to take on the new risk themselves. For those who move later in life, the change in risk level may not appear until the next generation. While underlining the complex relationship between environmental and genetic factors in determining who develops MS, these studies have also provided support for the opinion that MS is caused by early exposure to some environmental trigger in genetically susceptible individuals.

- **Gender:** MS is at least two to three times more common in women than in men, suggesting that hormones may also play a significant role in determining susceptibility to MS. And some recent studies have suggested that the female to male ratio may be as high as three or four to one.

- **Genetics:** Genetic factors are thought to play a significant role in determining who develops MS.
- The average person in the United States has about one in
- 750 (.1%) chance of developing MS.
- For first-degree relatives of a person with MS, such as children, siblings or non-identical twins, the risk rises to approximately 2.5-5% — with the risk being potentially higher in families that have several family members with the disease.
- The identical twin of someone with MS (who shares all the same genes) has a 25% chance of developing the disease. If genes were solely responsible for determining who gets MS, an identical twin of someone with MS would have a 100% chance of developing the disease; the fact that the risk is only one in four demonstrates that other factors, including geography, ethnicity and the elusive infectious trigger, are likely involved as well.
- Research has demonstrated that MS occurs in most ethnic groups, including African-Americans, Asians and Hispanics/Latinos, but is most common amongst Caucasians of northern European ancestry. Susceptibility rates vary among these groups, with recent findings suggesting that African-American women have a higher than previously reported risk of developing MS.

A new study provides further evidence of the potential long-term harms of head trauma, after finding that individuals who suffer a concussion in adolescence may be at greater risk of developing multiple sclerosis.

THE GIFT OF MULTIPLE SCLEROSIS

Concussion is a form of traumatic brain injury (TBI) caused by a sudden blow or jolt to the head, which can interfere with brain functioning.

- Signs and symptoms of concussion include loss of consciousness, dizziness, poor balance and coordination, changes in behavior and mood, memory problems, and confusion. Symptoms normally arise shortly after head injury, but they can sometimes take days to appear.

- While concussion symptoms are usually short lived, in recent years, research has shown that head trauma may have long-term implications for brain health.

- One study reported by *Medical News Today* in 2015, for example, found that professional football players who experienced concussion were more likely to have memory impairments in later life than those who did not suffer concussion.

- Now, researchers have identified a link between concussion in adolescence and later-life multiple sclerosis (MS) risk.

- Lead author Prof. Scott Montgomery, of Oerebro University in Sweden, and colleagues recently reported their findings in the *Annals of Neurology*.

Concussion and MS: Studying the link

- MS is a neurological disease estimated to affect around 2.3 million people across the globe.

- The condition is believed to be triggered by an abnormal immune response, wherein the immune system mistakenly attacks and destroys myelin, which is a fatty substance that protects nerve fibers in the central nervous system.

- For their study, Prof. Montgomery and colleagues used data from the national Swedish Patient and Multiple Sclerosis registers to identify 7,292 patients with MS. All subjects had been born from 1964 onward, and MS diagnoses were made between 1964 and 2012.

- Each patient with MS was individually matched by sex, year of birth, age at MS diagnosis, and place of residence with 10 people who did not have MS. In total, the study included 80,212 participants.

- Using data from the Swedish Patient Register, the team also identified any diagnosis of concussion among the participants during childhood (between birth and the age of 10 years) and adolescence (between the ages of 11 and 20 years).

MS risk increased more than twofold

- The team found no association between concussion in childhood and the risk of MS in later life.

- **However, the study revealed that participants who experienced one concussion in adolescence were 22 percent more likely to receive a later-life MS diagnosis, while the risk of MS was increased more than twofold for those who suffered more than one concussion.**

- Previous research has indicated that trauma to the head may prompt an abnormal immune response that damages the brain.

THE GIFT OF MULTIPLE SCLEROSIS

The authors speculate that this process might explain their findings.

"Head trauma in adolescence, particularly if repeated, is associated with a raised risk of future multiple sclerosis, possibly due to initiation of an autoimmune process in the central nervous system. "

- Prof. Montgomery says that their findings provide "another reason to protect adolescents from head injury, particularly where they are at risk of repeated trauma, including from sports-related injuries."

- As per the Centers for Disease Control and Prevention (CDC), in 2012, a diagnosis of concussion or another form of TBI was made in around 329,290 individuals in the United States who were treated for sports- or recreational related injuries.

Reference Sources

Who Gets MS?: National Multiple Sclerosis Society

Teenage concussion linked to later risk of MS - Medical News Today

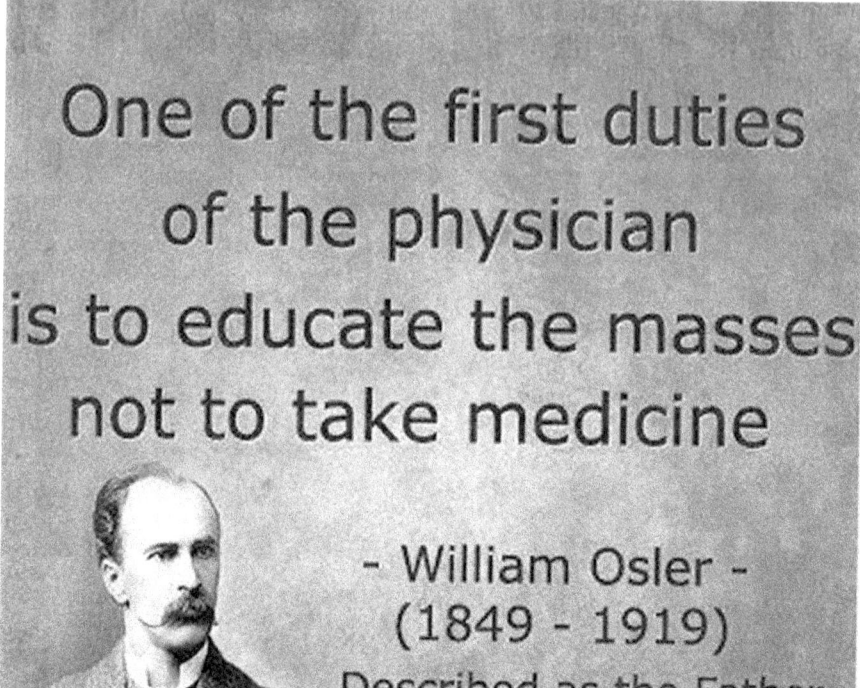

www.ingramcontent.com/pod-product-compliance
Lightning Source LLC
Chambersburg PA
CBHW052040300426
44117CB00012B/1901